DISCLAIMER

The *Art of Digital Hustle* is for educational purposes only, dropping knowledge to help you level up in the digital game. But let's keep it real—the author isn't giving legal, financial, medical, or professional advice. The content in this book is drawn from various sources and is intended to inspire, not replace, a professional's guidance. Reader before trying any techniques shared here, consult a licensed professional to ensure legitimacy.

By reading this book, you agree that the author isn't responsible for any direct or indirect losses that might come from using the info, including any errors, omissions, or inaccuracies. Read to comply with all applicable regulations and laws, whether international, federal, state, or local, including those related to professional licensing, business practices, advertising, and other relevant areas. The author and publisher aren't taking any responsibility or liability for the reader or purchaser of this book. Any perceived slight of an individual or organization is unintentional—we're all about good vibes here!

My Writing Inspirations, My Father Suhas Dixit, and

My Daughters Varnika Dixit and Sanika Dixit

ART OF DIGITAL HUSTLE

A Self-Made Map for Gen Z in Corporate IT

Convert Passion Into Purpose

#Self-help Improvement Book

AALOK DIXIT

ISBN
Paperback 979-8-89961-618-1
Hardcase 979-8-89961-631-0

This book is dedicated to
my beloved mother, Sarita Dixit,
whose soul rests in eternal peace.
And to all generations, forever young in spirit.

CONTENTS

Contents

FORWARD

BY HEMANT DESHPANDE

Building A Vibrant Community Of Purpose-driven Coaches | Ex-IT Leader

In 2014, after nearly two decades in the corporate world—including roles with global giants like IBM and Infosys—I hit a wall. The long hours, endless calls across time zones, and the creeping emptiness despite all the external "success" had taken a toll. I remember missing my son's second birthday because I was buried in a client escalation. That day, something inside me shifted. I knew I had to stop running on someone else's treadmill and start defining my path.

That decision led me to coach. It led me to a purpose. Moreover, it reminded me that success isn't just about climbing a ladder—it's about choosing the right wall.

That's precisely why *Art of Digital Hustle* is a book this generation needs.

In a world where digital careers are evolving faster than college curricula can catch up, where mental health struggles often hide behind high-performing LinkedIn profiles, and where the word "hustle" has been both over-glorified and misunderstood, this book offers not just perspective but a path.

Aalok doesn't romanticize the chaos of tech. He acknowledges it and equips the reader with a mindset, a compass, and the courage to navigate it. His MAP framework—Mindset, Adaptability, Purpose—isn't just a catchy acronym. It's a lifeline, especially for Gen Z and Alpha, who enter the workforce without rulebooks and guarantees and sometimes without mentors who understand their world.

What I admire most about this book is its soul. It doesn't preach from a pedestal. It shares from the trenches. Aalok's story of pivoting across technologies, learning fast, failing fast, and staying grounded resonates with every professional who's ever felt like an impostor or questioned if they were "doing it right."

This is not a "how to succeed in corporate IT tech" manual. It's a profoundly human, brutally honest, and refreshingly actionable guide to building a meaningful digital career without losing yourself.

To all the young professionals, coders, designers, product folks, and dreamers reading this.

Let this book be your reset button.

Let it remind you that you're not just building code, careers, or credentials. You're building character. And that's the most valuable asset in this ever-changing digital playground.

You don't have to hustle blindly.

You don't have to follow outdated scripts.

You can lead with clarity, heart, and a whole self intact.

Read this book. Reflect. Highlight. Apply.

And most importantly, stay true to yourself.

Because that's the real art of the hustle.

—Hemant Deshpande
Founder, HD Career Coaching
ICF-PCC | Mentor Coach | Former IT
Program Leader turned Purposeful Coach

PREFACE

THE ART OF DIGITAL HUSTLE—A ROADMAP FOR THE NEXT GEN

It's 11:48 AM IST on Monday, May 19, 2025, and as I sit down to pen this preface, I cannot help but think about the journey that led me to write Art of Digital Hustle - Don't Be Naïve, True to Self, Sharp in Mind—a Self-Made MAP for Gen Z IT Tech to convert Passion into a Purposeful IT Career.

This book is not just a guide—it is a vibe, a call to action for Gen Z and Alpha readers who are ready to take the tech world by storm, all while staying true to themselves. If you are a digital native dreaming of turning your Passion for tech into a career that slaps, you're in the right place. This book is your MAP—Mindset, Adaptability, Purpose—to hustle smart, not hard, and carve a path that's 100% you.

I have been where you are. In my early days at IBM, on Day 17, I was a nervous junior technician facing a visit from a senior database administrator (DBA). My "3rd Nutty Child Syndrome" had me spiraling—I thought I had messed up big time. But I had been building in public on DBA-Village.com, and my scripts and white papers had earned me mad respect. That day, I went from panic mode to the "Informix Guy" on the project floor, proving that visibility and authenticity can open doors faster than any job title. That moment sparked my mission: to help the next generation thrive digitally without getting lost in the noise.

The tech world in 2025 is a wild ride. A 2024 Gartner report states that 65% of tech skills expire within three years, and 84% of Gen Z prioritize purpose over pay (Deloitte, 2023). You are not here for the old-school grind—you want freedom, impact, and a career that vibes with your values. But the pressure is real, and the algorithm pushes FAANG goals, senior dev titles, and startup clout. That is where this book comes in. It is not about copying someone else's glow-up but crafting your own. Through stories like Dhruv "D" Carter's GreenStreak journey (from startup dreams to a 50K-user recycling app) and some visibility hacks, you will see how to stack skills, build in public, and define success on your terms.

The Book dives into building a skill stack over chasing titles, staying curious to avoid getting stuck, and hustling digitally while keeping your mental health in check. You will learn to create your MAP—Mindset (practical steps for Growth Mindset and staying true to yourself), Adaptability (How to adapt as per situation and handle change), and Purpose (how to avoid feeling lost and turning passion into an purpose). Whether you are freelancing, indie hacking, or just starting, this book is your guide to thriving in tech without losing your soul.

So, Gen Z and Alpha fam, let's hustle smartly. Create your own MAP, and turn tech passion into a career as lit as your favorite Spotify sound.

ACKNOWLEDGEMENT

I want to thank my wife, Aarti Dixit, for her unwavering support, which has enabled me to perform my best. I am grateful to her for all her support in the highs and lows in my life.

I want to thank my sister, Mayura Paranjpe, a clinical psychologist, her daughter, Srushti Paranjpe, and her son, Dhurv Paranjpe, for reviewing the initial content. I would also like to acknowledge my brother-in-law, Niranjan Adgaonkar; my dear friend, Sameer Dumbre; and his sister Dr. Swapnili Karmore; and her daughter, Swarnima Karmore, for their sincere feedback and invaluable input.

I also want to thank all those who have contributed to my life directly or indirectly, including my athletic coach, Rajendar Khandal (Raju Sir); my ideal Col. U V Deshpande; my Motivator Balasaheb Desai, and my cousin sisters, Nupura Dixit, Prachi Godbole, and Prajakta, all my friends and relatives, for their support and blessings.

Thanks to my Big Brother, Sagar Dixit, who is always there to provide support and encouragement.

Sincere thanks to Dr. Manjunath M S. (Mind Coach) for their support, wisdom, and the CBL community, which motivated me to author this book.

Finally, I want to thank Hemanth Deshpande (ICF-PCC, Mentor Coach) for motivating generations to read this book.

INTRODUCTION

With an accomplished career spanning over 24 years in the IT industry, Aalok has deep expertise in IT infrastructure management services across diverse sectors, including Retail, Insurance, Manufacturing, and Telecom. His global experience includes working in the US, UK, France, Ghana, and India, bringing a rich perspective to managing complex IT environments.

Aalok started as an Oracle DBA and gradually transitioned into leadership roles—Infrastructure Lead, Data Center Lead, and eventually Delivery Manager—overseeing people management, IT governance, and customer stakeholder management. Aalok has successfully led onsite and offshore delivery centers, driving stability and innovation across IT operations.

He is passionate about collaborating across teams to mentor and coach, building high-performance team cultures. He has a strong, grounded, and practical governance approach that is result-driven. He has consistently focused on delivering reliable and stable IT transformations and support.

On a personal front, he is an athlete at heart—formerly an Athlete (High Jumper) during his college days—and he made a comeback in 2019 at the "Master Athlete Federation Meet, "earning a bronze medal in the state-level Masters 40+ age category event. He is a yoga practitioner and practices mentoring coaching out of a passion for helping young IT professionals maintain their own physical and mental well-being.

WELCOME TO THE DIGITAL HUSTLE (WITHOUT THE BURNOUT)

"You were told to hustle, but unfortunately, no one warned you that the digital hustle might hustle you back"

– Aalok

Welcome to The World of job seekers or job creators—where opportunity moves at the speed of an update, but so does pressure in this AI-W (Artificial Intelligence -World).

You're entering an industry where yesterday's coding language or technology is today's legacy skill, and everyone's chasing "impact" but burning out in silence.

And if you're feeling excited and overwhelmed simultaneously— *trust me, you're not alone.* I have been there not as Gen Z/Aplha or Millennials but as Gen X. I think we are responsible for reducing the gap and confusion of today's connected World.

The reason I feel so is because GEN-Xs are the generation who are fortunate to see the evolution firsthand.

This book isn't here to add to the noise. I understand there's an overload of information out there, and I want to help you navigate it.

Think of this book as a map, guiding you through the complexities of the tech industry.

You are the generation with a lot of reasons. Questions, let's start with:

Why this book? And why now?

Because the old playbooks are breaking down, and Gen Z & Alpha are smart enough to see them.

The traditional advice for a tech career—climb the ladder, stay loyal, work hard, and wait your turn—but may not align with the World you're entering.

You need a different, agile, human strategy built around your unique identity and values. This is your career, and you have the power to shape it.

Gen Z and Alpha are entering a **"post-traditional" work era, one in which** identity, freedom, and purpose matter more than just a paycheck.

The old hustle culture (grind, burnout, overwork) isn't built for sustainability, and it's failing this generation.

The World of tech has changed—permanently.

AI is not the future. It is the present.

Work is not where you go; it is what you create.

And the old success formulas—college degree, résumé, corporate loyalty—although important, no longer guaranteed Growth or Success.

So, where does that leave you?

Right at the front of a revolution—but without a clear MAP.

Then, what is the way forward?

Try drawing your MAP to navigate and continuously correct the course as it progresses.

It is not important where you have started; it is critical to your direction.

This book has three key parts that will help you outline –

Right Mindset,

Right Adaptability and

Right Purpose, as 'Your North Star.'

To keep you on track using your own Operating System (OS) – **YOURSELF!!**

Core Concepts That Slap for Gen Z

Digital hustle ≠ is not chaos. It's about *intentional, flexible, self-led* career building—on your terms.

It's about understanding the fast-paced, ever-changing nature of the tech industry and learning to adapt and thrive in it.

You're not just "starting a job." You're entering a hyper-digital, AI-augmented, remote-first, creator-led tech economy.

The pressure is real—imposter syndrome, comparison, burnout. But so is the **Opportunity**.

Gen Z/Alpha reports the highest levels of burnout, even in early careers. Traditional hustle culture promotes urgency, constant work, and competition.

But young tech talent today is more value-driven, well-focused, and emotionally intelligent.

No one can give you a fixed path, but this book helps with **MAP** (Mindset, Adaptability, Purpose) to sustain and be **Resilient.**

What does "Don't Be Naïve and True to Self, Sharp in Mind" mean?

It's a reminder to maintain enthusiasm and optimism in the tech industry, be prepared for the unexpected, and always have a backup plan.

Let's delve into a hilarious and straightforward tale I heard a few years back that perfectly encapsulates the tech industry.

It's the 'Tale of Two Coders and a Very *Brave Printer*'.

Ravi – Fresh out of college. All high energy, zero error handling.

Sneha – Five-year senior developer. Dry humor. Deep scars from past deployments.

And their boss? Mr. Sharma speaks only of Jira tickets. Mysteriously feared. Possibly part of a printer. Maybe.!! 😊

During Ravi's first week at *CodeNest Tech*, he barges into the dev bay, grinning like he discovered console.log.

Ravi: "Sneha, guess what? Mr. Sharma told me I'll own the microservice next sprint!"

Sneha (not looking up): "Did he also give you prayer beads?

You'll need those when it crashes at 1 AM."

Ravi: "No, no, he said I'm *empowered*. End-to-end ownership!"

Sneha: "Aww. You still believe in unicorns and work-life balance. That's cute!"

Cue the infamous Tuesday afternoon. Mr. Sharma's printer dies. Mid-client demo. Smoke. Panic.

Mr. Sharma (panicking): "Why is this printer spewing '404 Page Not Found'? It's a hardware device!"

Ravi: "Uh… sir, I *might've* accidentally deployed a test script to the office network… It pinged every device for a response…"

Sneha (laughing): "You DDoS'd the printer?! Ravi, welcome to tech. You just promoted a printer to junior backend developer."

Mr. Sharma (holding the smoking paper tray): "You crashed the WiFi, Ravi. My fridge is tweeting error logs."

The next day. Ravi survives the *Sharma Stare*. Barely.

Ravi: "So… owning a service is less 'heroic coder moment' and more 'surprise babysitting job'?"

Sneha: "Exactly, buddy. It's like adopting a pet snake. Cute at first. Then it bites. And you're still responsible."

One month later.

Ravi—Bags under his eyes, clinging to his coffee mug like a lifeline.

Ravi: "I fixed a bug at 3 AM. Sharma didn't thank me… but he *did* stop cc'ing Legal."

Sneha: "Proud of you. You've evolved—from **Naïve Intern to Semi-Functioning Realist.**

Now, tell me, what's the wisdom of the week?"

Ravi: "Don't be Naïve - Just stay true to yourself.

Understand this: "Empowered" often means "You're the fall guy."

Even your cleanest code can crash into a printer.

And never assume Sharma knows what a router does.

So, stay curious. Stay kind. And remember—*naïve dreams get debugged.*

But wise ones? They get deployed.

Being naïve today is not about a lack of intelligence—it is about trusting those degrees, job titles, or company names, which means career safety.

Tech changes fast, and careers in tech change even faster. The myth of the "Perfect Plan" is dead.

Real success comes from flexibility, self-awareness, and momentum.

That is why I came up with the MAP.

The digital hustle is not about grinding till 3 AM, chasing job titles.

I know you do not care about titles, or pretending to be someone you are not just to "Make IT."

It is about building a career that feels good inside, not just impressive on LinkedIn.

Because tech is not just code. It is chaos in a hoodie. It is printers with IP addresses. It is Sharma using 'Ctrl+Z' as a Recovery Plan."

The Moral of the tale is that in tech, *"Don't Be Naïve"* doesn't mean giving up your enthusiasm—just back it up with backups.

I know for you it is about

- *Working smart without selling your soul.*
- *Growing fast without breaking yourself.*
- *Becoming a leader without waiting for permission.*
- *Work is not worship for you, but a meaningful purpose.*

This book is your MAP to thriving in a dynamic, ever-evolving tech landscape while staying true to who you are. It's about working smart. It's about no compromising your values and growing rapidly without burning out. And stepping into leadership without needing anyone's approval.

For you, work isn't an altar of sacrifice—it's a meaningful pursuit that aligns with your purpose and passions. The current Young generation is born into a world of complexity, but also unparalleled creativity. You wield tools, instincts, and access that no generation before you could imagine. The rules of success have shifted, and mastering them gives you a unique edge. In today's tech world, challenges abound—rapid innovation, ethical dilemmas, and the pressure to adapt at breakneck speed.

My book will unpack these complexities, offering practical insights to navigate them with confidence. It explores four key global challenges facing Gen Z and Gen Alpha: technological disruption, which demands constant learning to stay relevant; work-life integration, where balance is redefined in a hyper-connected era; ethical leadership, requiring you to make principled decisions in ambiguous situations; and global collaboration, where diverse perspectives must unite for impact.

You'll learn how to leverage your own strengths, adaptability, creativity, and digital fluency to carve out a purposeful and meaningful career.

Understand this isn't just about surviving. The tech world; it's about shaping it or embracing your potential, staying authentic, and leading with clarity to create a future that reflects your vision.

Now, look at the World view on the four main border challenges with Gen-Z / Alpha generations –

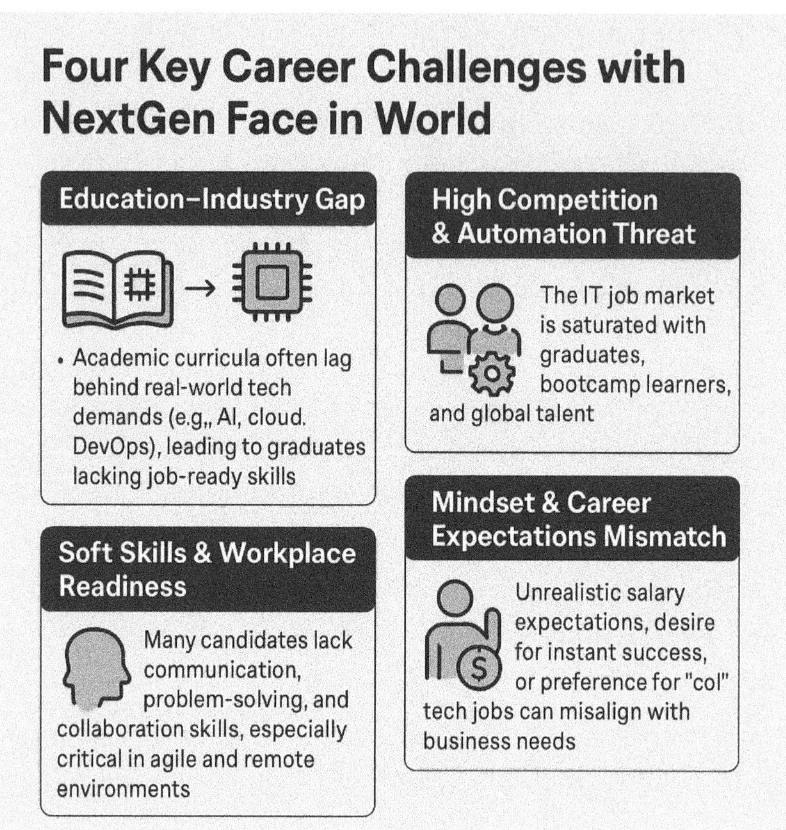

Four Key Factors of Career Challenges in the World

Education–Industry Gap - Certifications and hands-on project experience are becoming essential, but many candidates rely only on theoretical learning.

High Competition & Automation Threat - Simultaneously, entry-level roles (like testing or support) are shrinking due to AI and automation, raising the bar for freshers.

Soft Skills & Workplace Readiness—Employers now look for "T-shaped professionals" with deep technical skills and broad interpersonal abilities.

Mindset & Career Expectations Mismatch: Many struggles with persistence, adaptability, and accepting feedback—key traits in fast-changing tech roles.

After my interaction and my little study on Gen-Z/Alpha generation over the last few years, I have come to an understanding. The world is trying to resolve various general issues with Gen-Z / Alpha generations.

My observation is that the world of information overload causes negative and positive effects at a micro-subconscious level.

Post-speaking of young generations around me, this generation somewhere feels that at the bottom of their heart, something is not right with today's World, and old generation leaders and influencers are not taking responsibility with an open mind.

When Gen-Z / Alpha generations observe the Climate Change issue, the War on Terror, and terrorism, they have very biased views on geopolitics. They feel that the older generation is in denial and refuses to acknowledge the World's real problems, always treating only the Symptoms. They are convinced that baby boomers or Gen X are not taking responsibility for ground actions politically for problems like the Climate issue, as one example.

So, Gen Z/ Z/Alpha feels that listening to baby boomers or Gen X is a waste of time because, for them, it is a low-key lecture, even though it is good for them.

However, at the same time, the Gen-Z/Alpha generation is overly optimistic about a highly connected World. They really want to make a positive difference using digital means, whereas the Baby Boomers feel that it is a waste of time.

At the same time, Gen X feels that Gen-Z/Alpha should focus primarily on schooling and college first and avoid social media distractions as much as possible.

The millennial generation feels that social media is the only way to survive in the world in the future, especially after the 2020 pandemic.

Gen Z and Alpha are unsure about what's happening, but they believe social media and ChatGPT (OpenAI) are essential for their lives, like food. They prefer talking to digital bots, Alexa, Google Assistant, and AI assistants rather than humans.

The struggle between generations often leads to mental and emotional crises, which can be challenging to manage effectively.

Tell me, am I not telling the truth here?

I know that facial expression you are giving right now. Come on!!

Anyway, let's move on.

Honestly, I feel all older generations are responsible for reducing the gap between generations before it is too challenging to handle at home, in offices, and in our societies.

We must consider things and have candid conversations with the younger generations.

And try to see the World through their lens because Gen Z/Alpha is a Smartphone-Born generation.

Let us understand this with a scenario, if your phone battery drains out, what type of response or reactions will you get from different generations, based on research on the net, here is the view for your perusal -

"Battery Low!—How each generation reacts, *"If your phone battery drains, how you react… says more about you than your résumé."*

Whether your phone is screaming for juice at 2% or your life bar is hitting red from burnout, the reaction pattern tells a lot about your mental Operating System (OS).

Let's decode how each generation responds—boomers to Gen Z and Alpha—when the battery dies, and this metaphor secretly explains why listening is the ultimate hack for you.

Boomers (1946–1970): Why didn't you charge it before you left?

These are with "Pre-Charge Mindset."

- *Carry a power bank the size of a brick.*
- *Still owns a Nokia somewhere just in case.*
- *Thinks "20% battery" is a dead Phone.*
- *"Back in our day, we had landlines. You kids and your ding-ding-dings..."*

Morals: Prevention > Reaction. (Also, "Why didn't you listen to me?")

Listening Tip: Boomers believe listening is about *anticipating problems* before they arise. They prep. They plan. They *lecture*. If you listen, you'll avoid disaster.

If not, trust me, you'll get another low-key lecture that will drain you out. I hope you can relate to it, *right?*

Gen X (1971–1980). Great. Just great

These dudes are "Silent Meltdown Masters".

- *Won't show panic but starts sweating inside.*
- *Opens Settings > Battery Usage like it's CSI.*
- *Has a spare cable in the car from 2006.*
- *Blames the system, the app updates, and sometimes fate.*

Morals: Life's unfair, but we cope. Quietly. While looking for a charger.

Listening Tip: For Gen X, listening is about *internalizing and adapting*.

They expect the World to disappoint them, so they listen just enough to manage their expectations. They do not talk too much; they say what matters.

Usually, the Gen Z / Alpha approach avoids any lecture or sphere of negative energy and doubts. So, they listen to them to keep things in their pockets.

And whatever resonates, they keep it for the rest, just drop it from the mountain.

Millennials (1981–2000): I literally can't. Not now

Trust these guys are real "Emotional Response Experts".

- *"Omg, my life is falling apart" (because there is no Spotify in the gym).*
- *Panics, posts a story about a low battery before it dies.*
- *Knows all the ways to optimize battery, but still doesn't.*
- *"I need my phone—my therapist, bestie, and calendar."*

Morals: Everything's a *feeling*. Low battery = existential crisis.

Listening Tip: Millennials want to *feel heard*. Listening is emotional support.

Say, "That sucks" even if it's just 10% left. Validate them before offering a fix—bonus points for memes.

We must understand that this generation is born with smartphones, so it is a challenge for them to see life without smartphones and Gadgets.

Gen Z (2001– 2012): Ayo… I'm at 1%. Let's see how long it lasts 😺.

These are bits of "Chaos is the brand."

- *Lives life in airplane mode to "save battery".*
- *Gambles with 2% like it's Squid Game.*
- *Sends 37 memes with 3% remaining.*
- *"If I die, tell my followers I went out like a legend."*

Morals: Drama + humor = survival. Battery is a social experiment.

Listening Tip: Gen Z listens to *vibes*, not instructions. They *hear you* but are also scrolling on YouTube, installing Facebook, etc., while pretending.

Speak in punchlines. Use analogies. Show respect by not being boring.

Gen Alpha (2013–2030). Why doesn't it just charge from the air?

These are those who are Native to "Digital World Sci-Fi Brains"

- *Thinks "battery optimization" is broken tech.*
- *"Hey Siri, charge my phone." Then they stare in disappointment.*
- *Wants wireless everything now.*
- *Can reprogram a smart fridge but forgets to plug in their iPad.*

Morals: If it's not instant, it's outdated. Recharge = Mindset, not just cord.

Listening Tip: For Gen Alpha, listening is *interaction*. They ask questions *before* you finish your sentence. Make it a dialogue. Gamify it. Don't monologue. They tune out at "back in my day…"

So, what's the point here? Everyone freaks out when the battery drops. But how they respond, listen, learn, and handle stress is different. So, let's be respectful to each other.

And here is **my golden nugget** for you –

If you don't listen to the signals—from your phone or people—you'll burn out without warning because listening isn't passive. It's your charging cable to life. – Aalok

Does that make sense to you?

Now let's touch on today's young generation Mental Health Crisis Challenge and why it is not easy –

The Challenge: Gen Z and Alpha are the most open generation about mental health, advocating for therapy, self-care, and emotional vulnerability.

However, anxiety, depression, burnout, and loneliness remain widespread on social media.

Why It's Difficult: Social media pressure, economic uncertainty, climate fear, and constant connectivity contribute to stress.

While awareness is high, access to affordable and effective mental health care remains uneven in today's World, and social stigma still lingers in many cultures and communities.

Climate Change and Environmental Collapse

The Challenge: Gen Z is deeply concerned about the planet's future and advocates sustainability, activism, and corporate accountability.

Many are changing personal habits and calling out greenwashing.

Why It's Difficult: Real systemic change is slow despite rising awareness. Political inaction, corporate lobbying, and global inequality make it difficult for individual actions to scale into meaningful global impact.

Frustration grows as time runs out to reverse ecological damage.

Although it is challenging to get out of the loop of Mental Crisis due to information overload in social media, and because of already "Fried Dopamine" triggers, creating massive digital chaos in the mind.

The constant challenge of information overload and tasks drains positive energy from your daily IT career routine and impacts job performance, despite having good skills.

What is Dopamine-Fried Generations?

Let me share one story, where the neon haze of Metroplex, three in their 20s, navigated the 2025 grind, their brains buzzing from the endless scroll.

Cilly, a freelance UI designer, lived for YouTube and Insta clout;

Her phone was a slot machine of likes.

Kai, a DevOps intern, chased X notifications like they were paychecks.

Lila, a cybersecurity wannabe, doomscrolled Reddit, paralyzed by FOMO.

They were all Dopamine-*Fired Generation*—Gen Z, wired to crave instant hits from social media's candy store. Mornings at their co-working space were a circus.

Cilly, mid-Sketch file, kept refreshing her Reels analytics, muttering, "If this doesn't hit 10K, I'm cooked." Her designs were half-baked as her brain chased the next viral rush.

Kai, tasked with debugging a Kubernetes cluster, was too busy memeing on X about "cloud life." His boss's Slack pings went unanswered, drowned in a sea of retweets.

Studying for her CompTIA cert, **Lila** spiraled into a Reddit thread titled "Am I Too Dumb for Cyber?" instead of cracking her flashcards. Their jobs suffered, their vibes tanked, and their lives felt like a glitchy app stuck on loading.

One day, their co-working café's WiFi crashed, blessing or curse, they couldn't decide.

Cilly, cut off from her algorithm fix, panic-tapped her phone.

Kai groaned, "No X? How do I know I exist?" Lila, free from Reddit's abyss, stared at her laptop, lost.

Enter **Ravi,** the barista with a side hustle in mindfulness coaching.

"Y" all are dopamine junkies," he said, sliding them oat lattes.

"Social media got you chasing hits like it's Candy Crush. Your jobs, your life—they're collateral damage."

Ravi's words hit like a 404 error.

Quick Reality Check Stat - *A 2024 Pew study backed him up: 70% of Gen Z felt social media hijacked their focus, with 55% reporting job stress from digital overload.*

Cilly admitted, "I'm designing for likes, not clients."

Kai confessed, "I'm coding for clout, not commits."

Lila sighed, "I'm scrolling instead of studying."

Ravi dropped a hack: "Try a dopamine detox. One hour daily, no socials—just your work, your thoughts, your *why*." They took the challenge.

Cilly swapped Reels for wireframes, nailing a client pitch.

Kai muted X, fixed his cluster, and got a "clutch dev" shoutout.

Lila ditched Reddit, aced her cert prep, and landed a pen-testing gig. Their lives felt less like a lagging stream, more like a clean codebase. They still loved their apps but learned to log off and live on.

Social media's a slot machine, not your soul's Operating System (OS).

Log off, lock in, and code a life that's more than a scroll—because your absolute W's aren't in the algorithm, they're in you.

The key point is that Dopamine's a cheap high, fam—chase likes, and you'll lag; chase purpose, and you'll frag the game of life.

Market Trends - Gen Z / Alpha Job Professional

- *Deloitte (2023) found that 49% of Gen Z have changed jobs in the past 12 months, many citing purpose and mental health as key reasons for their digital hustle.*

- *Interesting Fact, according to Microsoft's Work Trend Index (2023), 52% of Gen Z are already considering job changes due to burnout, lack of growth, or misalignment with values.*

- *A Gen Z dev who got laid off after chasing the "perfect" FAANG job— but built a freelancing career and gained freedom.*
- *LinkedIn Skills with the highest growth rates are AI literacy, self-management, and cross-functional collaboration, not just coding or IT support operations.*

The key point is, what do you need as a NextGen IT professional?

Right Mindset, Right Adaptability, and Right Purpose?

In the coming section, I will personally walk with you with the utmost care to ensure you do not feel lost in managing the challenge of Digital Hustle.

CONCLUSION

Let's summarize what we have learned so far -

You understand key concepts about this book and what digital hustle is.

You learn about world challenges, the Dopamine-Fried Problem, and Mental Crisis.

You learn a bit about the generational gap and respect for generations.

You learn, you do not need another productivity hack.

You learn, Don't Be Naïve, and True to self, Sharp in Mind.

You need simple steps to gain clarity, confidence, and a strategy that will allow you to GrowUP without grinding yourself down.

The "Art of Digital Hustle" is about *flexibility, creativity, and speed* in a world where skills beat credentials. That's why this book exists— to help you hustle differently.

Smarter. Softer. Stronger - And let's build a career that fits *you.*

Not the system. Not someone else's definition of success.

It's time to hustle with MAP, but it is on your terms.

PART I

MINDSET—BUILDING YOUR INNER TECH CEO

Let me clarify: my conversation with you is going straight and bold. OK!!

I hope that's fine with you. You don't need a fancy title, a MacBook on a mahogany desk, or a startup in stealth mode to start thinking like a CEO.

In tech, your job title might say "Junior Developer," but what truly defines you is your **MINDSET.**

Before you lead a team, launch a product, or survive your first chaotic release, you've got to learn how to lead One Person: **Yourself!**

Let me share with you how I stumbled upon this realization—the slightly embarrassing way.

But I do not mind sharing it with you all. If you are reading this book, it means you are universally connected to me. It's a bit spiritual, but if you find it too intense, take a chill, breathe, and move on to the next section.

Let me rewind a few years with my experience as a 'Software Engineer' –

Here is the scene –

I joined IBM as a Software Engineer in 2004 and still treat my IBM ID card like a Hogwarts letter. 😊

It was Day 17 in the job—I was feeling sharp and ready to impress—when Mr. "Senior Manager with Zero Chill" walked up to me and said, *"Hey, quick task for the weekend, shouldn't take more than 2 to 3 hours."*

It took 48 hours countless cups of coffee, and all my faith in humanity.

It turns out that "quick task" was tech speak for - *Congratulations! You now own this undocumented mess, which was last touched during the Jurassic period. Good luck, Champ.*

By Monday, I was a walking zombie with a Git commit history and an existential crisis.

That weekend was my first lesson in digital hustle reality; It is not about saying yes to everything.

It is about thinking smartly, acting sustainably, and knowing when to protect your energy, like production data.

That was the moment I started asking myself a simple question-

"What would the CEO version of me do right now?"

And no, that version of me wasn't chilling in a corner office—it was probably somewhere debugging life, sipping cold chai, and setting boundaries like a boss.

Let's continue my IBM story in chapter one, where I'll share more about my experiences, challenges, and lessons learned.

Chapter one is about that mindset.

First, we'll discuss how to build your Digital Hustle Operating System (OS)—a Mindset that's smart, sustainable, and still hungry.

This system is about being strategic in your decisions, managing your energy and time effectively, and always staying hungry for growth and learning.

Then, we'll dive into something every early-career techie needs to hear-

Your first or second job and initial roles doesn't define you, but it will shape you.

So, if you're ready to stop reacting and start designing your tech journey like a leader, let's dive in. We're not just writing code anymore—**we're writing your career MAP.**

It means we will plan and strategize your career path, considering your skills, interests, and opportunities in the tech industry.

DIGITAL HUSTLE MINDSET—SMART, SUSTAINABLE, AND SELF-DRIVEN

"A professional Leadership & Careers isn't about titles—it's about building the right mindset from Day One of Your First Job."

– **Aalok**

DAY 17 DISASTER: THE TALE OF NOBODY BECOMES INFORMIX DBA GUY INSTANTLY

It was my 17th day at IBM. Just two weeks in and still behaving like the "new intern who thanks the water cooler."

I had my badge, my email was working (most days), and I had just figured out where the good chai came from in the cafeteria.

And then Enter: *Mr. Sharma.*

Senior Manager. Moved like a lion through the cubicles. His stare alone could refactor your code.

That day, Mr. Sharma stood in front of our war room with a face that said, "Something painful is coming." And then, he dropped it -

"We must migrate a legacy Informix database from SCO Unix to Windows 2000 Professional.

Who's in?" he announced, throwing us a curveball we never saw coming.

Dead silence. You could hear someone's playlist pausing in fear.

Everyone suddenly had invisible phones to check or shoes to tie. I, being young, eager, and dumb enough to want to impress, raised my hand.

My mistake was not hearing the word "Informix." My first lesson on poor listening led me into a trap.

You'd think I offered to catch a live snake with my bare hands.

Mr. Sharma squinted, pointed at me, and said the words I'll never forget:

"Ah, we have one strong man in the room."

He clapped once. "Done. You'll get the details over email."

Me: "Uh, sir—what's Informix—?"

Too late. He had already disappeared into the jungle of cubicles like Batman.

My teammates turned slowly toward me with "RIP" written on their faces.

"Why did you raise your hand, bro? Nobody uses Informix anymore!"

"All of us are Oracle guys! That system is ancient!"

"This is career suicide. Good luck."

Two of them even backed away from me physically, like I'd just caught a contagious disease.

"Don't expect much help, OK? We seriously don't know that tech," they warned, leaving me to navigate this daunting task alone.

Despite the overwhelming odds, I mustered a weak smile.

"No worries… I'll figure it out," I vowed, determined to turn this seemingly impossible task into a learning opportunity.

I had no clue what I was doing.

That evening was rough. Panic, Google searches, half-understood documentation, and one recurring thought - *"Why didn't I just fake a phone call like everyone else?"*

The next morning, I brewed some extra-strong coffee, took a deep breath, and typed my dump question-

"How to understand Informix for someone who only knows Oracle."?

Hours flew by. I found a rare "One Migration Guide on Informix Database" PDF—a gold mine! I downloaded it excitedly and hit "Print" to get eight pages.

Guess what, I sent the print request for 800 pages.

Second lesson: Do not panic when you are in the middle of a hustle. OK!! Keep a note.

My luck was so great that the office printer in the middle of the hall, right next to Mr. Sharma's cabin, started churning like it was launching a rocket.

Papers everywhere. Printer overheating. Sounding like a fax machine from hell.

I bolted to the hall, paused the printer, and saw Mr. Sharma standing by the door, arms crossed, watching the chaos with an expression that screamed "who hired this guy?"

Me (nervously): "Sorry, sir… honest mistake. Just needed eight pages. I've… stopped it."

He said nothing. Just stared. I was three years old.

But I didn't quit. I collected my mountain of papers, found the eight pages I needed, and returned to the task like a man on a mission.

Armed with the migration guide, I figured out the database structure. I used Oracle knowledge to reverse-engineer a plan:

- Using the guide, after studying the source Informix DB running on the UNIX platform, create an identical database and tablespace structure in the installed Informix DB on the Windows 2003 Operating system.

- Then, I created a blank table structure without data and FTP from UNIX to the Windows server.

- Then, I created an insert script statement with data, and it made a 150 GB file, which I FTPed from UNIX to a Windows server.

- I used Informix's DbExport / DbImport utility and installed the table structure in the newly created DB. I ensured all DB parameters were set to the same setting, from UNIX to Windows, whatever was applicable. Then, I installed the insert script using the utility and started praying that nothing caught fire.

Sounds easy. (It wasn't.)

I built a schema. Scripted the inserts. FTP'd everything over. On Saturday at 3:00 AM, I was the only soul in the office. Even the security guard stared at me like:

"Bro… get a life."

I passed out on the chair. When I woke up on Sunday morning, the copy/import process was still running, and I had no clue if it was working.

By Sunday evening, doubt crept in.

What if it failed?

What if the data was corrupt?

What if Mr. Sharma was sharpening his "termination sword"?

But something inside me said:

"Don't touch it. Don't panic. Just wait."

Monday morning.

Copy process completed. I opened the new Informix database on Windows. Ran a simple record count.

Those three seconds were my Longest. Three. Seconds. Ever.

Then—boom! All 150 GB. Every row. Every byte.

I fist-pumped the air like I had just launched a satellite.

I fired off an email like a Rocket.

The migration was completed successfully. Screenshots are attached.

I need support to connect the DB to the application, which I am not aware of, but I am ready to learn."

Mr. Sharma replied:

"Good. Well done."

That's it. "Well done."

The biggest project of my life so far… and two words. But hey, I'll take it.

The moral of the Story is that in the world of tech, courage is sometimes just *saying yes* before you know how and then learning like your career depends on it.

Don't be naïve. But don't be afraid either

Raise your hand, even if you don't know everything. Just don't send 800 pages to the office printer.

Because sometimes, the best way to stand out...

It is to *mess up big, recover, and deliver like a boss.*

Let me decode the formula for you: What does digital Hustle mean?

Let us understand what digital hustle means and why it's not just a rebrand of burnout. Because if you don't design your path, someone else will.

"Hustle" used to mean grinding until your eyes bled. Now it's time to redefine it—before it defines *you.* The digital Hustle isn't about working more hours or saying yes to everything.

It's about creating a career path that's self-led, purpose-driven, and sustainable—using digital tools, communities, and mindsets to fuel intentional growth, not endless output.

Let me break down the key concepts that make things simple for you.

Digital Hustle = Smart + Self-Directed + Sustainable

What is Smart?

- You use tech to accelerate, automate, and amplify.
- You're not working harder—you're working *sharper.*
- Example: Using AI tools like Notion AI, GitHub Copilot, or ChatGPT to speed up learning or daily workflows.

Remember - *Use the tool as a reference and add your fresh perspective.*

What is Self-Directed?

- You build your career like a playlist—customized, evolving, and entirely yours.

- You learn via YouTube, Discord, peer groups, side projects—not just what your boss or university says. Start doing it now.

Remember - *You're not waiting to get picked. You're building your stage.*

What is Sustainable?

- You design routines and goals that energize, not exhaust you.

- You make space for mental wellness, creativity, and non-linear growth.

Now, let's compare the Hustle of the old and digital generations.

Old Hustle	Digital Hustle
Grind harder	Learn faster, adapt smarter.
Climb the ladder	Build your own bridge.
Burnout = badge of honor	Burnout = red flag
Follow the rules	Know the rules, but rewrite your own
Work to impress others.	Work in alignment with yourself

The point is to understand here. You don't need to follow a broken system to prove your worth.

Your digital Hustle is your personal Operating System—flexible, futureproof, and built to evolve with you.

Let's try some examples now, because you must have been thinking what the heck this guy is talking about:

- *Let's say a 22-year-old builds a personal brand on LinkedIn and lands freelance work from DMs (Direct Message) without applying to jobs.*

- *A coding student learns Python through Twitch live-streamed sessions and starts selling automation scripts.*

- *A junior designer uses AI tools to scale their portfolio 10x faster, while taking weekends off.*

The Hustle is not dead—it just got smarter.

Moreover, it belongs to *you* now, and you can control it.

But do you know what the actual hustle starts when the college announces that companies are coming to campus for interviews? That feeling of happy butterflies, but at the same time, the mind gets anxious, too.

Well, ask yourself a question?

IS YOUR MIND SELF-TALK HUSTLE CREATOR?

I keep all that self-talk in mind. I need the best company, the best role, and my dream job.

Slowly, I start the self-hustle pattern and loops, comparing myself with other friends' selections and placements.

Sometimes, these hustles get too much in and drain you out.

But let me tell you this, I know it will resonate with you –

"Your First Job Isn't Your Whole Life Story."

So, do not have to be negative in your self-talk that - "You're *not stuck—actually you're starting.*"

As Napoleon Hill said in his books –

"You can't change where you started, but you can change your direction. It is not what you will do but what you are doing now that counts."

So, be chill. See yourself with an open mind, viewing each opportunity as a raw diamond whose job it is to shine. Be the go-to person whom people can trust.

There is a famous quote from John C. Maxwell that keeps me going even today in my IT job-

"Go–to Players are the people who find a way to make things happen no matter what. They don't have to be in familiar surroundings. They don't have to be in their comfort zone."

So, the thing is, **your first job isn't your destination. It's just your *sandbox*—a place to experiment, observe, and grow.**

In tech, where skills evolve monthly and roles shift quickly, your career isn't a straight ladder—it's a web of opportunities. And the first role you take? It's just one node.

This is called "Open for Mindset Shift."

A couple of Mantras to Encounter Negative Self-Talk, which helped me:

"You Become What You Think About," by Earl Nightingale.

"Your enemy is not going to harm as much as your thoughts, Kept Unguarded"

– by Buddha

LET ME CLARIFY A FEW MYTHS HERE AS NUGGETS FOR YOU

Your Title ≠ Your Identity

- You might start as a QA tester, helpdesk intern, or junior dev—but that doesn't define your future. The most successful tech pros often begin in roles they later pivot away from. Identity should be tied to who you're becoming, not just what's on your email signature.

So, note that "Your job is what you do. Your *path* is what you build."

Learn the Game Before You Redesign It

- First jobs give you more than tasks—they teach you how teams communicate, how deadlines get pushed, and how leaders act. Learn how the "machine" works, not just your keyboard.

Focus on systems thinking, observe how problems flow, who makes decisions, and what habits lead to growth.

Your First Job Is a Launchpad, Not a Life Sentence

- Don't overcommit to being "on track." There is no single track in tech. Side projects, learning communities, certifications, freelancing—all help reshape your path.

Use your first job to test what you *enjoy*.

Let me share a few Real-World Examples that I have come across

- *A front-end dev who pivoted into UX after realizing they cared more about how things felt than how they rendered.*

- *A support analyst who used downtime to learn automation became the team's RPA expert.*

- *A Gen Z intern who built an internal tool to solve a minor problem— and got fast-tracked into a product role.*

CONCLUSION

Your Digital Hustle Starts Now, Yo! Gen Z and Alpha.

You've just been handed the cheat codes to the digital Hustle— smart, self-directed, sustainable, and straight-up *You*.

The Story of Mine Day 17 Disaster proves it, success in IT is not about knowing everything.

it's about saying "Yes" to the grind, learning fast, and recovering from epic fails like a boss.

You are not here to chase titles or burn out for clout—you are here to code a career that's as fiery as your favorite playlist.

Let's wrap this up with a MIND MAP to lock in that digital hustle vibe and some action steps to make it stick.

Mindset: Say Yes, Then Stress**

My 800-page printer fiasco was peak chaos, but I owned it.

Quick Stat - *A 2024 LinkedIn study says 68% of Gen Z land gigs by embracing challenges over credentials.*

Your vibe? Be the rookie who raises their hand, even if you're Googling "Informix" at 3 AM.

Remember - *Courage isn't knowing the code—it's committing to debug your way to glory.*

Adaptability: Pivot Like a Pro**

Tech's a moving target—new stacks, roles, and chaos. I pivoted from Oracle to Informix over the weekend.

Quick Stat - *A 2023 Stack Overflow stat shows 70% of devs learn a new language yearly. Stay nimble, fam. Learn fast, fail faster, iterate fastest.*

Remember - *Adapt or get 404'd—your Hustle's only as dope as your next pivot.*

Purpose: Make It Mean Something**

I did not just migrate a database; I proved it was clutch.

Quick Stat - *A 2024 Deloitte survey says 84% of you want jobs with impact. Tie your Hustle to a *why* freedom, community, saving the planet. That's the fire that keeps you coding.*

Remember - *Hustle without purpose is just noise—code for a cause, not applause.*

So, don't just hustle for the Gram—code a legacy that crashes the basic servers and shakes the algorithm.

However, do not be hard on yourself and don't obsess over landing your dream job right away.

Instead, focus on building the version of *yourself* who can recognize—and create—the dream job when it appears through small, persistent, atomic steps.

One thing to do is to get over your worrying habit

Using the simple practices framework of 30, 60, and 90-day plans called out in this book will help you greatly self-reflect on what is working for you or what is not working, and provide feedback.

The key point here is that your first job isn't to prove you're ready. It is to help you get ready and warm up for what's next on your terms.

In the next chapter,

let's explore the topic of "Your First Job Doesn't Define You—But It Will Shape You", how you can craft your own path at entry level, and what mindset is required to encounter today's Digital Hustle.

Remember—*your first job's just a sandbox, not a script. Code your Hustle, own your failures, and build a career that slaps. The MAP is yours—run it.*

Activities to Lock In the Vibe for You

Hustle Hack Challenge: *Pick one IT skill (e.g., Python, CSS) and commit to 30 minutes daily, weekly. Post progress on X with #DigitalHustle.*

Mindset Journal: *Write down one scary tech task you've dodged (e.g., a hackathon). List three steps to tackle it. Start one today.*

Purpose Vibe-Check: *DM a friend on Discord: "What's one world problem you'd code a fix for?" Brainstorm a project idea together.*

Chapter 2

YOUR FIRST JOB DOES NOT DEFINE YOU—BUT IT WILL SHAPE YOUR MINDSET

"Your title is temporary—it is your identity that lasts. Consider your role as a training ground for your higher purpose and goals.

– Aalok

IN THE BEGINNING, I AM IN MY DREAMS, WELL....., ALMOST!

Before, I had one goal: to land a job in IT—Infosys, IBM, Oracle, or anything that sounded like I would make it big enough to put "Tech Enthusiast" on my biodata.

Instead, I got hired as an intern at a chartered accountant firm in Nagpur while pursuing my PG in parallel.

Yep! I had no introduction to computers back then.

Dusty files, clunky calculators, and strong coffee were enough to wake your ancestors.

Then, one day, a miracle happened, the firm bought one computer—actual it is a PCs!

I still remember those legendary Windows 486 (3.1) PC (Personal Computers) machines. They sat in boxes for a week like ancient artifacts. No one dared to open them.

There *was* a manual, but in the office, it may as well have been written in Latin. Everyone waited for a vendor to come, like summoning a digital priest for a PC puja.

Then came the plot twist, a new intern joined—*the* computer girl. She was certified and trained.

Let's just say it's not hard on the eyes. Interns got excited—until we all found out she was married, which was an instant mood crash. But she knew tools we'd only heard of in legends: Lotus-123 and FoxPro. (Google them, kids. Or just ask me—I'm basically ChatGPT for the 90s—he he he!!.) I know it is a bad joke.

She became the firm's unofficial tax-report queen.

Interns lined up like pilgrims to get their reports done.

Me?

I was a shy third-born introvert suffering from "Middle Intern Syndrome." I did not dare cut the line or ask for favors. My clients were calling. My CA boss was glaring. And my tax reports? It's still handwritten like it was in 1947.

Then one day, another PC arrived.

I lit up like Diwali. I thought, "Finally! Another assistant is coming!"

Nope. The next day, the boss called a meeting:

"Due to budget issues, there will be no second assistant. Interns need to figure it out by themselves.

And do not overload the current assistant."

Basically: Figure it out or suffer. Oh!! What the Heck?

So now we have a brand-new PC, but no one to use it, no budget for classes, and no intern brave enough to even press the power button.

Until *she* came up to me—yes, the computer girl—and asked, "Hey, hey! Hold, do not jump to conclusions here. OK!!

There was a situation where the office boy was out. She said, "Can you plug this in? Cable for me"

Me (internally screaming): MY MOMENT HAS COME.

I entered the "computer lab" (read: one room with AC and a table), and I swear the cool air felt like a trip to Kashmir. She handed me a piece of paper with cable instructions on how to plug it, and I asked her, "You are the expert, right? You know this stuff?"

She smiled nervously.

"Honestly, I only know how to log in and use two tools. Setup and wiring? Not my thing.

The vendor charges too much, and Sir is not ready to pay if he wants to use the second PC, so… I looked around, saw you staring at the ceiling, and figured you were available."

Touché. Oh!! OK, then I helped her set the PC cables. Then I made a small request.

"Can you teach me to create my tax reports?"

She paused.

"Are you trying to steal my job?"

"NO! I want to *learn about computers*, that's all.

Help me, and I will take over some of your tasks. You can log it in your timesheet like you did."

She blinked.

"Wait… you are saying *I get paid* for your tax reports, and in return, I teach you?"

"Exactly. Call it my 'training fee.'"

Moreover, just like that, my IT career began—inside a dusty CA firm in Nagpur, bartering tax reports for knowledge.

Within months, I was pulling reports myself—mind you, not for love of tax but because I had fallen for something else entirely: computers.

That job never made it to my LinkedIn, but it taught me what no degree could:

- How to lead without a title
- How to solve problems without formal training
- **How to stay consistent—even when no one is watching**

Quick Stat- *91% of Gen Z feel pressure to succeed early (LinkedIn, 2023). Nevertheless, success is not landing a fancy title on Day 1—it is building small, real skills that compound fast.*

My intern stipend was ₹500/month. No bonuses, no benefits—just bitter tea and priceless life lessons:

- *Speak up when it is scary*
- *Learn even when no one is paying you*
- *Build habits that outlast the job title*

Trust me, in 2 to 5 years, you will forget your job title. And you will *never* forget the Mindset its Built.

So, Embrace Humility Over Hype

Your first job might be far from glamorous. You might debug legacy code, reset passwords, or help customers with basic queries.

That is OK.

That is where the real lessons live—in the small, often overlooked tasks that teach patience, grit, attention to detail, and communication under pressure.

Think of it like your "career bootcamp."

You are not just getting paid; you are getting paid to learn—how to show up, speak up, and level up.

Look at a few Real-World Stars: From "Lowly" to Legendary

- *Satya Nadella, Microsoft's CEO, began his career as a technical marketing engineer, not a developer or product visionary. He learned how to sell, explain, and simplify tech.*

- *Kevin Systrom, founder of Instagram, started as an email marketing intern at Odeo (the company that became Twitter).*

- *Arlan Hamilton, a venture capitalist, began homeless and worked odd jobs before breaking into tech investment, proving that titles can't measure trajectory.*

The key question here is, what did they all have in common?

They treated every role like it mattered—and it did.

Diverse First Jobs: Unlikely Launchpads, Few Real-World

Your first job does not need to be your dream Job or company—or even in tech or non-tech—to shape your future success.

Some of the world's top entrepreneurs and IT and non-IT leaders started in places you'd least expect:

- ***Ramdev Baba** (Co-founder of Patanjali Ayurved Limited) is an Indian multinational conglomerate known for its products in Ayurveda, natural health care, and consumer goods. He co-founded it with Acharya Balkrishna in 2006.*

- ***Jeff Bezos** (Amazon) – Worked at **McDonald's** as a short-order line cook in high school. He credits it with teaching him about automation and systems thinking.*

- ***Susan Wojcicki** (former YouTube CEO): She started **marketing and writing,** and then rented her garage to Google's founders. That experience eventually led her to join the team and become one of the first employees.*

- ***Dr. Manjunath M.S.** (founder of Brain Accelerator) is a platform dedicated to enhancing cognitive abilities through programs in speed reading, memory techniques, emotional intelligence, and mind mastery. As a leading Mind Performance Coach in India, he has trained over 50,000 individuals, including professionals, business owners, and students, to optimize their mental capabilities.*

- ***Stewart Butterfield** (Slack co-founder) – His first job was designing **websites for friends and small businesses** as a freelancer, long before Slack existed.*

- ***Jan Koum** (WhatsApp co-founder) – Worked as a **janitor at a grocery store** to support his family after immigrating to the U.S. He later taught himself computer networking at a public library.*

- ***Melanie Perkins** (Canva CEO) – Taught **Photoshop classes to students** in her free time. The pain she saw led to the creation of Canva.*

- ***Padmasree Warrior** (CEO of NIO U.S., former CTO of Cisco) – Began as a **chemical engineer intern**, not in software, proving that pivoting is part of the journey.*

- ***Hemant Deshpande** (founder of HD CC) is a distinguished career and leadership coach based in Pune, India. He has over 25 years of global corporate experience, including IBM, Infosys, and Cisco roles. He is an International Coach Federation (ICF) certified coach specializing in career transformation, executive coaching, and leadership development.*

What is the Key Takeaway here?

Your Title Is Not Your Trajectory.

My stories have reminded me throughout my career that the value of your job lies not in prestige *but in perspective.*

What matters most is your willingness to extract growth, no matter what the setting?

Cleaning tables? You are learning workflow and people skills.

Retail? You are building communication under stress.

Freelancing? You are gaining independence and problem-solving.

The key point is that every job has a hidden curriculum.

The only question is—*are you paying attention?*

Quick stats that smash the Myths from your mind

- *72% of professionals say their current role is not directly connected to their first job title (LinkedIn, 2023).*
- *40% of IT professionals say their first role felt "underwhelming," but 85% credit it with teaching them the core habits that built their long-term success (CompTIA Career Path Survey, 2022).*
- *The average Gen Z worker is expected to switch roles up to 10 times before age 35—your first role is just step one.*

So, listen with care, Show Up Like It Matters—Because It Does

Your attitude in your first job sets the tone for how others see your potential.

Are you someone who only performs when it is "cool" or someone who learns, leads, and listens—regardless of the title?

The fastest way to unlock doors in your career is to outgrow your current position, not by complaining but by contributing, learning, and improving.

Quick Stat on Career Development & Skill Building (Emphasize in First Jobs)

- *83% of professionals say their first job taught them critical soft skills—like communication, problem-solving, and time management—that they still use today. (National Association of Colleges and Employers (NACE), 2023)*

- 70% of hiring managers value practical experience (even in unrelated fields) over perfect academic credentials for entry-level IT roles. (*CompTIA Workforce Study, 2022*)

- Less than 27% of professionals work in a field directly related to their first job.—*(LinkedIn Career Path Survey, 2023)*

- Nearly 50% of IT professionals say their first job was outside the IT sector, but it helped them build tech-adjacent experience or people skills that proved critical later.—*(Dice Tech Sentiment Report, 2022)*

- Millennials and Gen Z who took on early leadership or initiative (even in small roles like shift leads or team trainers) were 3x more likely to be promoted within their first 3 years.—*(Gallup: Early Career Development Study, 2021)*

- *People who felt supported and challenged in their first jobs reported 2.5x higher career satisfaction over the next decade.—(Harvard Business Review, 2022)*

- *The average Gen Z worker is expected to hold 10–14 jobs by age 38.—(U.S. Bureau of Labor Statistics, 2023 Projection)*

Remember - *"Your first job is less about prestige, more about positioning—to learn, grow, and test your capabilities in the real world."*

Now, picture this: you are fresh out of college, heart pounding as you enter your first IT gig.

Maybe you are a QA tester staring at endless bug reports or a helpdesk intern rebooting routers while dreaming of coding AI.

The vibes? Equal parts hype and panic.

You are chasing that "dream job" aesthetic, but real talk, Gen Z and Alpha: your first job is not your forever—it is your *forge*.

It does not define who you are, but shapes how you think, hustle, and grow.

Like my Informix saga, it is where I learn to say "yes," mess up, and level up.

Your first job is a sandbox, not a cage.

Quick Stat: A 2024 Glassdoor study says 65% of Gen Z switch roles within two years, proof that they *are not locked in.*

That helpdesk gig?

It teaches systems thinking—how teams sync, how deadlines flex.

That junior dev role?

It is your crash course in debugging under pressure.

Every task, failure, and "why am I here?" moment codes your mindset for the long game.

Quick Stat: A 2023 Harvard study found that *80% of successful IT pros credit early jobs for grit and adaptability, not titles.*

Take Maya, a 21-year-old who started as a data entry intern.

Boring? Sure.

But she used downtime to learn SQL, build a dashboard for her team, and pivoted to data analytics by 23, earning $95 K.

Her mindset—treat every role as a hackathon—turned a "meh" job into a launchpad.

Your first gig is not your identity; it's your training arc.

So, lean in, soak up the chaos, and code a ready mindset for anything.

Now, look at how to chart a Path from an Entry-Level Career—Without Losing Yourself?

The hustle of older generations, like Baby Boomers, is about survival.

The *digital hustle?*

It's about Strategy, Sustainability, and self-leadership. You're not here to run faster in someone else's race but to design your own game.

One built on clarity, curiosity, and conscious action.

With the right mindset, tools, and routines, you do not burn out to break through—you build systems that help you grow without putting yourself through *the process.*

You are not chasing a title—you are crafting a trajectory.

You are not waiting for a break—you are building leverage.

Moreover, you are not stuck—you are just getting started.

The truth is that hustle is not dead. It just leveled up—and now, it belongs to you.

So, before you dive deeper, ask yourself –

What would it look like if my hustle felt good, and what works?

Next, we'll unpack *"Your Path from Entry-Level to Lead—Without Losing Yourself"* and explain why it's not just a rebranded grind.

We will break the myths, decode the mindset, and help spot the traps that keep people busy but not better.

This is not about doing more. It is about becoming more *on your terms.*

You don't need to wait for 10+ years, get five promotions, or manage a team of 20 to start acting like a leader.

The best growth and to be a leader in tech today are often makers, builders, and collaborators who started by leading themselves, their mindset, habits, and choices.

So, please don't just build a resume; build Authority, Reputation, and Trust.

We will discuss how to build authority more deeply in the upcoming chapters.

Before crafting your path, let's understand- What is the key tension point here?

You want to win, but not at the cost of your well-being or identity

Trust me, FR, I am not a person to give you low-key lecturing here, OK!!

As you read my book more, I will give you simple but mind-provoking ways, daily affirmations, and easy-to-use tools and techniques.

Let's say you still feel that NAAAA!! It is too overwhelming to practice.

I also have one (SSt) Single Secret Technique that you must try. As called out in the final chapter, it worked for me even today. If not all techniques, one or two will work for you.

Let's Understand What is Changing in the Job World?

I will be direct with you in my conversation now, so do not take it personally.

You are free to agree to disagree. I have no plan to sugar-quote anything because I know Gen Z / Alpha like grounded conversion - *"Just come to the point, Man!" Right? Or "Get to the point, fam!"*

Tech no longer needs just coders—Yes, you heard me.

It needs Creative, Emotionally Aware, Multidimensional People.

More Human skills like storytelling, resilience, and empathy are now **"Power Skills."**

Just being Good and hardworking at your Job ≠, Staying Relevant.

You need to grow across disciplines.

I have been in the information technology industry for the past 24 years and have experienced how the demand for human skill sets has evolved. Here's a quick view: the DOT COM BOOM in 2000, the introduction of Cloud in 2005, the Smartphone / iPhone revolution from 2008, Cloud getting solid ground in 2015, and Hybrid Cloud getting traction in 2020.

We are already in the initial phase of the Gen-AI revolution starting in 2025.

THE EVOLUTION OF COMBINATION SKILLS

2000s

Web developers with business acumen

Hard Skill: HML. JavaScript, ealy ECommerce platfors
Soft Skill: Business understanding, adaptability

Developers who could also understand user needs and market behavior became the backbone of early internet startups.

2008
SMARTPHONE REVOLUTION

Mobile app developers with UX focus

Hard Skill: JOS/Android development. APIs
Soft Skill: Design thinking, empathy for useexprience

Those who combined coding skills with empathetic design thinking built more engaging, user-friendly apps.

Lesson: Tech is togɪ impact lies in emotional connection with the user.

2015
CLOUD MATURITY

Cloud engineers with collaboration & DevOps mindset

Hard Skill: AWS. AZure, CI/CD, Infrastructure as Code
Soft Skill: collaboration, continuous learning

Teams shifted from sileed sysadmins to ofalborative DevOps culture. Those who couid communicate across teams thrived

Lesson: Tech moves fast—who learn fast and collaborate move faster.

2025
GEN-AI ERA

AI practitioners with critical thinking & ethics

Hard Skill: LLMs, prompt engineering. AI toolsintegration
Soft Skill: critical thinking, ethical judgment, creativity

In an ers of AI co-pilots, professionals who can guide AI with judgment and creativity will lead innovation.

2000s – Dot Com Boom: The Rise of Web Developers with Business Acumen

Hard Skills: HTML, JavaScript, early eCommerce platforms

Soft Skill: Business understanding, adaptability

Why it worked: *Developers who could also understand user needs and market behavior became the backbone of early internet startups.*

Lesson: Tech was valuable, but *storytelling and business sense* elevated careers.

2008 – Smartphone Revolution: Mobile App Developers with UX Focus

Hard Skill: iOS/Android development, APIs

Soft Skill: Design thinking, empathy for user experience

Why it worked: *Those who combined coding skills with empathetic design thinking built more engaging, user-friendly apps.*

Lesson: *Code is logic, but impact lies in the emotional connection* with the user.

2015 – Cloud Maturity: Cloud Engineers with Collaboration & DevOps Mindset

Hard Skill: AWS, Azure, CI/CD, Infrastructure as Code

Soft Skill: Collaboration, continuous learning

Why it worked: *Teams shifted from siloed sysadmins to a collaborative DevOps culture. Those who could communicate across teams thrived.*

Lesson: *Tech moves fast—those who learn fast and collaborate move faster.*

2025 – Gen-AI Era: AI Practitioners with Critical Thinking & Ethics

Hard Skill: LLMs, Prompt Engineering, AI tools integration, Power App with AI, Power Automate with AI

Soft Skill: Critical thinking, ethical judgment, creativity

Why it works: *In an era of AI co-pilots, professionals who can guide AI with judgment and creativity will lead innovation.*

Lesson: *AI may automate tasks, but human wisdom adds purpose.*

The key point is that we are at the edge of a multiple skills demand market.

So, many skill combinations will give you leverage to level up your game in the Job Market. I am not able to give all the combinations in this book.

However, I will try to give examples to ponder on, and if you want more help, you can reach me *at the email address (DIXITUSA303@ GMAIL.COM).*

Now let us understand using some examples -

Few Suggestions

- First by Default Skills for today's World for any newcomers in IT- my recommendation is to Complete an external Certification, preferably, or at least get trained online or offline on Fundamentals on Cloud tech for a minimum of three to four of them (Microsoft Azure, Amazon AWS, Google GCP, and Oracle OCI)
- Second By Default Skills for today's World for all newcomers In IT - Complete external Certification preferably or at least get trained online or offline on Gen-AI Fundamentals at least three to four of them from the list offer by – Microsoft (Co-pilot), Open AI (ChatGPT), Google Gemini (formerly Bard), Amazon Bedrock, Meta-AI)

Must do (Examples)

- Microsoft – AI Skills Challenge + Azure AI Engineer Certification (AI-102)-

Focus: Azure OpenAI, model deployment, real-world AI scenarios.

- Google Cloud: Generative AI Learning Path -

  Focus: Gen-AI foundations, LLMs, Prompt Engineering, Vertex AI

- AWS – Machine Learning Path with Gen-AI Labs-

  Focus: Gen-AI tools on AWS (Bedrock, SageMaker), LLMs

Good to do (Examples)

- Prompt Engineering for Developers – OpenAI & DeepLearning. AI –

  Focus: Practical use of prompts for OpenAI APIs

- DeepLearning.AI – Generative AI Specialization-

  Focus: Text generation, diffusion models, prompt engineering

Quick Handy Tips for Skill Combination to Ponder

- *Focus on prompt engineering, LLMs (like GPT), and hands-on projects. Try to earn certificates with labs or mini projects—pair certification with GitHub projects, LinkedIn posts, or a portfolio site.*

- *Aim for roles like Prompt Engineer, AI Assistant Developer, Gen-AI Product Tester, Large Language Model Trainer, Natural Processing Language (NLP), AI Ethical Process and Analytics (Non-technical), or IA Ethics Principal Expert.*

- *A hybrid role (Azure Cloud PaaS + Windows Admin or Linux + Terraform) requires a combination of skills for migration-type projects.*

- *Aim Skill Combination (Hybrid Azure Cloud + AVD + FinOps) is a great combination to stand out in the job Market.*

- *Follow other young Gen Z creators to see how they do this (YouTubers, indie app devs, explainers) and influence products and culture without traditional resumes.*

Quick Mind Map to show skills combination on how to become job-ready, one simple example

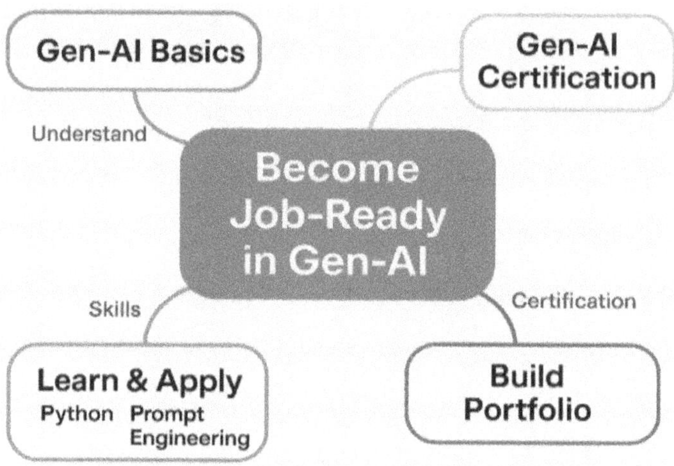

"Continuous Learning & Upskilling is the ONLY Persistent Motivation in Life."

– Aalok

Try this activity and start smart with your learning journey

Get yourself registered in ChatGPT's free version or paid version as you wish, use the following prompt, which helps you to give very high-level details, and start a Gen-AI learning journey:

> *ChatGPT, can you suggest some compelling structured plans to head start my Gen-AI learning journey [Focus on prompt engineering, LLMs (like GPT), and hands-on projects. Try to earn certificates with labs or mini projects. Pair certification with GitHub projects, LinkedIn posts, or a portfolio site. I want the In table format [Share URL for top 5 Gen-AI Fundamental Courses List] and resonate with [Gen-Z and Gen Alpha Generation in year 2025 and beyond]."*

Note: Feel free to tune the prompt for the desired outcome.

Gen-AI Learning Plan (2025). - 6-Month Structured Roadmap

Month	Focus	Learning Goals	Resources	Prompt Engineering for Developers – OpenAI & DeepLearning.AI	Showcase Actions
1. Foundations of Gen-AI & Prompt Engineering	Grasp AI basics, LLMs, and prompt engineering. Learn to craft prompts that slap.	Understand LLMs (e.g., GPT, LLaMA) and their mechanics (transformers, attention). - Master prompt engineering: zero-shot, few-shot, chain-of-thought. - Get comfy with Python basics for AI	Course: DeepLearning. AI's "ChatGPT Prompt Engineering for Developers" (free, 2 hours). …. - Course: Google Cloud's "Introduction to Generative AI" (free). - Tool: Play with ChatGPT or Hugging Face's playground. - Read: "Attention is All You Need" paper (simplified summaries on YouTube).	Project: Build a simple chatbot using ChatGPT API (e.g., a Q&A bot for your fave game). Push to GitHub. - Certificate: Earn DeepLearning.AI's prompt engineering cert. - Mini-Project: Write five prompts for different tasks (e.g., summarizing, translating) and test them.	GitHub: Create a repo for your chatbot with a README.md, flexing your prompt logic. - LinkedIn: Post about your cert with a meme: "When your prompt makes GPT sing ♫ #GenAI." - Portfolio: Start a free site on Vercel to log your projects.

Note: For Full Output, Try Yourself on ChatGPT using the suggested Prompt.

Top 5 Gen-AI Fundamental Courses

Course Name	Provider	Why It Slaps	URL
ChatGPT Prompt Engineering for Developers	Deep Learning.AI	Free, 2-hour course with Jupyter notebooks to build a chatbot. Taught by AI legends Andrew Ng and Isa Fulford.	DeepLearning.AI
Introduction to Generative AI	Google Cloud	Free intro to LLMs and responsible AI. Includes labs on Vertex AI for prototyping. Perfect for cloud-curious Gen Z.	Google Cloud
Generative AI with Large Language Models	Coursera (Deep Learning. AI)	Deep dive into LLM mechanics with Python labs. Build summarizers and more. Cert boosts your resume.	Coursera
Prompt Engineering for ChatGPT	Vanderbilt University (Coursera)	Teaches prompt crafting with real-world tasks (e.g., social media posts). Cert for your LinkedIn glow-up.	Coursera
Mastering Generative AI (6 Weeks)	Constructor Academy	Hands-on course with Replit and Hugging Face projects. Build AI apps and learn ethics. Portfolio-ready cert.	Constructor Academy

Remember—your first job is not a life sentence—it is the tutorial that unlocks your main quest. Do not let a title trap you—*it is the commitment that builds your backend for a legendary IT glow-up.*

CONCLUSION

Your First Job—A Mirror, Not a Mold. Your first job is not your destination—it is your proving ground.

It will not define the professional you will be for life, but it will reflect the Mindset you are starting with.

Whether fixing broken code at 3 AM, accidentally DDoS'ing a printer, or surviving your first terrifying client call, you are doing more than "working."

You are learning to handle chaos with curiosity, pressure with grace, and uncertainty with courage.

You will be tempted to think, "Is this all there is to tech?"

However, trust me: it is just the trailer, not the movie. What truly matters is not your Title or your tech stack—it is the Mindset you carry forward:

Are you adaptable?

Are you learning?

Are you still raising your hand, even when it is scary?

If the answer is "yes," congratulations—you are already shaping a career that you, not your job title, will define.

So let the job shape you—but never let it shrink you.

The best careers are not built from day one; they are debugged, improved, and continuously deployed. So, you do not have to wait for things to do passionately or for a promotion to become a leader.

You can start now—lead **to learn and Start Crafting your Own Path, show up, and help others. That is the real hustle.**

Furthermore, it is how you rise without losing who you are.

Activity

Skill Sprint: *Pick one Skill from your job (e.g., scripting) and spend 10 hours mastering it via YouTube or freeCodeCamp. Share progress on #BuildInPublic.*

Systems Map: *Draw a flowchart of how your team works (who decides what, who codes what). Spot one process to improve and pitch it.*

Pivot Plan: *List three roles you would love (e.g., AI dev, UX designer). Find one free course or community to start exploring.*

Chapter 3

START CRAFTING OWN PATH, STAY TRUE

An IT Tech Career is not about fitting a Mold; it is about consistently and courageously showing up as the best version of yourself.

– Aalok

THE BACKBENCHER WHO HACKED HIS WAY TO IT

Yo, Gen Z and Alpha, gather 'round for a real one.

Here you go. There is a real me as a certified backbencher in school, vibing in the chaos of Nagpur, India, circa the early 2000s.

Think of *Taare Zameen Par*—that kid who stares out the window while numbers and letters do somersaults in his brain? That was me.

Math? A circus.

English? Not my cup of tea.

Questions? Oh, I had plenty, but raising my hand in class?

Nope, my arms were on strike.

I still kick myself for that—missed shots, fam.

Fast-forward to undergrad, I'm scraping by in Commerce, not because I loved it, but because my friends were doing it.

Peer pressure's a sneaky algorithm, y'all.

My one flex? Athletics. I was a high-jump beast, repping my university at All-India level four years straight and snagging gold at the 2000 Ashwamedh state comp.

And soaring over bars while my grades were barely clearing the ground. Post-grad rolled around, and I'm in a Commerce PG program, still clueless about my *why*.

Academia was giving the "side quest" energy, not the main storyline.

That's when the vibes shifted during an internship at a Nagpur firm. Messing with tax reports and a clunky computer PC sparked something.

I was like, "Wait, PCs are kind of dope." But I am a non-tech Commerce kid.

That's like trying to speedrun Dark Souls with a broken controller.

Enters Prachi, my cousin and resident genius.

She says, "Yo, try my Java class at this computer institute. The first week's free; if it slaps, I'll convince Mom and Dad to cover the fees." I'm sweating.

Prachi, I'm not an engineer. Commerce and coding? That's oil and water."

She just smirked, "You'll figure it out."

I didn't. Java class was like facing Ambrose's bouncers—code flying over my head at 90 mph.

The instructor likes, "Learn C++ first." So, I tried C++. Same vibe—bouncers, no bat.

The C++ teacher says, "Bruh, start with C." I'm stuck in a tutorial hell loop, telling Prachi, "I'm coding in circles!" She's unfazed, signing me up for a six-month C, C++, Java, Oracle, and Visual Basic crash course.

I'm juggling PG, internship, and 4 a.m. high-jump practice—my day? 4 a.m. to 11:30 p.m., fueled by optimism and positive vibes. Gen Z, you'd call it a "grindset montage," but I was just tryna!! Not flop.

I sucked at programming. Got decent marks in the course, but coding wasn't my jam.

But Oracle? That clicked.

I thought, "Databases are simple—learn the architecture, memorize commands, and you're golden."

LOL, my first database assignment yeeted that myth into the void. (Story for another day.)

The point is that I listened to my gut. Programming was a big no, but Oracle felt right. Staying true to myself was the absolute W. I went all-in, bussing to Pune for Oracle 8i certs—five exams, four months, pure hustle.

My Nagpur study squad, a crew of non-tech dreamers like me, kept the vibes high. We were the underdogs, coding our comeback.

Now, the job hunt.

Since there were no campus placements, I took a rogue approach with the "Cold Resume" start.

Picture me, a commerce kid, handing out 500+ resumes anywhere I saw the word "computer" on hoardings. A lot of them throw paper at me, but that is OK!! I am mentally prepared for everything.

Consulting gigs? Flops.

Rejections? A whole collection.

But I had a plan. I'd scour *The Hitavada's* job listings every Wednesday, spotting patterns like a data analyst. October? Java and VB jobs. January? Data modeling. February? App testing.

My gut screamed, "March or April's gonna be Database Admin season." My squad thought I was wild, but I'd studied a year's worth of ads like it was my Oracle certs. I bet on it, packed a bag, and landed in Pune with a 30-60-90-day plan -

- **30 Days**: *Spam resumes in every computer-related spot. Big companies ghosted me, so I hit up institutes.*
- **60 Days**: *Pivot to accounting or auditing (my Commerce backup).*
- **90 Days**: *In the worst case, sell credit cards—easy money back then.*

I didn't need 60 days. Within 30, I snagged a faculty job teaching Oracle. My gut, my grind, my *unwavering determination* paid off.

I was not an engineer but crafted my path by staying true to what resonated with me—databases, not code.

It took courage to follow my gut, and I want to pass on that lesson to you, Gen Z and Alpha.

Your journey is a custom playlist, not a default algorithm.

Listen to your gut, hustle through the chaos, and don't let "I'm not X enough" gatekeep your glow-up.

Lessons That Slap

Ask Questions, Even If You're Shy: I regretted staying quiet in school. Please raise your hand, DM that mentor, and post it on Discord. Questions are your XP. Don't be afraid to ask; it shows your curiosity and eagerness to learn.

Your Gut's Your GPS: Programming wasn't my vibe, but Oracle was. Trust what feels right, even if it's not the 'cool' path. Your instincts are your best guide; following them can lead to your true calling.

Hustle Smart, Not Blind: My newspaper starts and 30-60-90 plan weren't luck—they were data-driven bets. Study patterns, make moves.

Fail, But Don't Fold: 500 resumes, countless nos, one yes. Keep pushing. Every L's a commitment to your comeback.

Action Steps for You

Gut-Check Journal: *Write down one thing you love (e.g., gaming, design) and one IT skill that vibes with it (e.g., UI/UX, cybersecurity). Explore it for a week.*

#CraftYourPath Post: *Share a "What's my IT vibe?" post on X or LinkedIn. Tag a skill you're curious about and ask for resources.*

Cold Resume 2.0: *DM three IT pros on LinkedIn with a short, "I'm learning [skill], any tips?" Most won't reply, but one might change your game.*

Remember—don't *let the algorithm pick your playlist. Craft your IT path with gut, grit, and a sprinkle of chaos, and watch your backbencher arc go viral.*

Leading an IT Career without authenticity leads to burnout, anxiety, and impostor syndrome -

It is critical to stay connected to

- *Your values (Integrity, Ethics, Respect, Honesty, Responsibility, Kindness)*
- *Your boundaries (Freedom, Say-Do Ratio, Authenticity, Morals)*
- *Your Purpose (Holistic View, meaningfull, Contributing to large Good)*

Create a Self-Made Map for Your IT Career

*Career design > Craft a career path, create a Vision Board, or use **My PCB Method.***

The goal is to have a living, visual tool for reflecting on, planning, and evolving your tech career *without losing who you are.*

Before you create MAP, warm up your Mind for Clear n' Clean intent setting:

- **Own your time**: Use tools like time-blocking or deep work sessions.

- **Reflect often**: Weekly reviews, journaling, or retros help track growth. *(Use of **DFW Method** called out in this chapter)*

- **Stay grounded**: Know your values so you are not chasing someone else's version of success.

Remember - *Carefully understand that your ability to say "no" to things that don't align is a leadership trait, not a liability. Always aim to build influences with contributing intent.*

How to Build Intent with Influence, Not Just Skills

- Be the person who connects the dots across teams. The key trait is necessary to connect the dots with teams and people to develop and practice EQ (Emotional Intelligence).

- Share your learning journey publicly (LinkedIn, Twitter, GitHub). Sharing your learning doesn't mean sharing your secrets with the world; on the contrary, you demonstrate the key attitude of "*Sharing is Caring*" to the world.

- Start mentoring someone one step behind you—even if informally. This is one step toward creating your leadership brand in the long run.

Key Facts: *The Harvard study found that emerging leaders are defined more by how they support collaboration than by technical superiority.*

Now, delve into the Self-Coach Formula using the DFW Method (Or *Decluttering Framework*):

Let me introduce you to my two techniques. You can try both or either one of them, but honestly, my recommendation is to start by trying both for 30 – 60 – 90 days and longer to realize a significant change in your ways of thinking, simplify your approach and decision-making about your career, and rewire your subconscious level.

The first one is the DFW Method, or "Decluttering Framework," which helped me during my struggles and routine by keeping my mindset grounded and staying true to myself.

I know what you are thinking at this point. I have been there - I know practicing and writing a Journal or diary sounds a bit old-fashioned, but trust me, if you can use it offline or online, Excel or Google Sheets, etc, it will give you a candid view about yourself to reflect, trigger ideas, and build resilience to bounce back effortlessly, provided you are making it a regular habit –

Job Reflection Check-In" (a mini exercise): Every 30 to 60 to 90 days, ask:	Honest Date Wise Personal Tracker (Example)			
Key Question	Date →	Date →	Date →	Date →
What am I learning?				
Programming Skills, Tools, Tech	Shell Scripting, PostgreSQL, Python, Jason	Oracle DBA	RHEL	DevOps / AI
Communication and Giving Status Updates	Lean and effective Email Communication	Completed self-paced training on communication.		
What drains me (My Ds) vs. what energizes me (My Es)?				
D- No new learning,	Fixing the same bugs daily			
D - Rigid 9–5 work schedules	No flexibility or autonomy.	The meeting requested that the challenge be shared with the lead.		

E- Working on AI-driven apps or creative solutions	AI Certifications Level Target completed on 31st May	Request Voucher		AI Certifications Level 2 Target completed on Aug 30th.
E- Remote/hybrid work with purpose-driven projects that align with their values (like sustainability or social impact).	Deliver High Quality Project Working Remotely.	Share the Lesson proactively	Learning about Time Management	Leading Emotional Intelligence & Effective Communications
What more do I want in my next opportunity?				
Purposeful Work, Creative Freedom, Flexibility & Autonomy, Inclusive Culture,	Happy with Flexibility & Autonomy, but not satisfied with not having Creative Freedom	Share feedback with HR.		
What help do I need for my next opportunity?				
Guidance for Growth & Learning	Support for Creative Freedom and Pointers Skill Upgradation	Plan Cloud FinOps Certification		
Not Soft training, Human Attitude training for Blissful Work Culture	Request for Mentor to Project Manager for self-improvement	Attended the First session with the Mentor		

Bounce-Back Blueprint using PCB Method

Oh, Ya!! I know engineers…. What are they thinking?

This PCB is not a "Printed Circuit Board." However, it can be done if you have the means to do so. ☺

Let me introduce you to a **"Personal Career Board" (PCB Method)**—a living document where you map skills, values, experiments, and goals.

Let us learn HOW TO USE IT

Tools: Excel, Word, Simple Diary to note, or use tools like Notion, Canva, Miro, etc.

Time: *Update monthly or quarterly. Check in weekly if using it as a habit tracker.*

Vibe: *It is a mirror, not a scorecard. You're not failing—you are building.*

There are 6 Sections in PCB

WHO I AM—My Values & Vision

"What matters to me, and what does success look like on my terms?"

Prompt	My Example – Use *or replace the following text to create your PCB*
Core values	*Time Freedom, creativity, impact, Fitness, wellness, self, and others, live true.*
Purpose (in one line)	*Through my actions and positive behavior, I aim to develop technology that assists real people in solving real problems and reduces work stress in the workplace.*
Ideal future self	*A calm, confident tech lead building tools for startups I care about.*

WHAT I CAN DO—My Current Skill Set

"What do I know? What am I learning? What do I want to master?"

Skill Category	Skills I Have	Skills I'm Building
Tech	*HTML/CSS, Python, Oracle, Azure Cloud*	*Docker, React, GitHub, GCP*
Soft	*Communication, problem-solving,*	*Negotiation, team leadership*
Tools	*Figma, Notion, VS Code*	*Postman, Jira, ServiceNow*

HOW I LEARN—My Learning Pipeline

"What am I learning this month? How am I learning it?"

Focus Area	Resource	Time Blocked
JavaScript Fundamentals	*freeCodeCamp course*	*Mon/Wed 7–8 PM*
Career Clarity	*Book: "So Good They Can't Ignore You"*	*Sundays*

Note: Add a "Done" column to track completion.

WHAT I'M TRYING—Experiments in Motion

"What am I testing, building, or exploring?"

Experiment	Why it matters	Status
Building a portfolio site	*To showcase my dev skills*	*In progress*
Contributing to open source	*To build confidence and community*	*Started*
Cold DMs on LinkedIn	*To get career conversations started*	*Scheduled*

Rule: At least 1 "experiment" per quarter.

WHO I CONNECT WITH—My Support System

"Who are my people? Who inspires me? Who can I learn from?"

Type	Name / Platform	Action
Mentor	*College alum on LinkedIn*	*Ask for a 20-minute call*
Peer group	*Discord dev community*	*Share progress weekly*
Role model	*Sara Vieira (developer, speaker)*	*Follow and read the blog*

You don't hustle alone. Build your circle. This is similar to studying in a group in college days.

WHERE I'M HEADED—Short + Long-Term Goals

"What am I aiming for? What does 'progress' look like to me?"

Timeframe	Goal	Why it matters
1 month to 3 Months	*Complete my first freelance gig*	*Real-world experience*
3 months to 6 Months	*Apply to 3 companies I admire*	*Clarity on where I belong*
In 1 year	*Land a full-time remote tech role*	*Freedom + income stability*
2–4 years	*Become a team lead or indie builder*	*Impact on my terms*

Before concluding this chapter, let me ask you this

Are You Ready to Play the Long Game Without Burning Out?

Think of the seasons: Sprint when needed, but pace yourself.

Protect time for creativity, rest, and curiosity—that's where leadership ideas are born.

Don't over-identify with your job—leading yourself requires *perspective,* not just effort.

Are You Ready to Design Your Career Like a Product?

Dare to Experiment: Try distinct roles or projects inside your company (or outside it).

Collect Critical feedback: Ask peers and mentors what they notice about your strengths.

Keep Iterating: Your version to lead project efforts will change—and that's a good thing.

I hope your answer is a resounding YES to all the questions, as it signifies your readiness to level up your game.

Embracing a growth mindset is crucial for your IT career journey

Now, say this Mantra Loud with me, come on, don't hesitate, and practice daily.

Example (I, Aalok, am Comfortable In Uncomfortable Situations.)

I <Name> am Comfortable in Uncomfortable Situations.

I <Name> am Comfortable in Uncomfortable Situations.

I <Name> am Comfortable in Uncomfortable Situations.

CONCLUSION

Let's be real—there's no GPS for success in IT. No perfect roadmap, no guaranteed playbook. But here's the good news: you don't need one.

You need a compass—your mindset, curiosity, and a strong sense of *why you started.*

Crafting your path as a self-made IT pro isn't about waiting for the "right" opportunity or the "perfect" mentor. It's about making small, smart moves.

Learning on weekends. Saying yes to the scary task in week two. Googling until 2 AM. Asking dumb questions (they're not dumb, by the way). And most importantly, it's about staying true.

True to your grit.

True to your learning.

True to the fact that nobody knows everything, but someone who keeps going eventually figures it out.

This is your journey, and staying true will lead you to success. You don't need to be a genius; you just need to be consistent.

Start now.

Start messy.

Move Fast.

Learn Smart to Adapt.

But Start True, Because the best IT careers are not handouts—they're **Hand-Crafted**.

PART II

ADAPTABILITY—
MOVE FAST, LEARN SMART

In the digital age, it's not your title that gets you hired—it's your ability to deliver across domains that sets you apart.

– Aalok

Yo, Gen Z and Alpha, let's talk for a sec.

Imagine you're at a networking event or chilling in a Discord server, and someone asks you the classic, **"What do you do?"**

If you answer "I'm a junior developer" or "I'm a data analyst," you're selling yourself short, fam.

In 2025's digital hustle culture, your job title's just a label, like a default avatar in a game.

But here's the real power move - Your skill stack- the unique combo of what you know, what you can do, and how you solve problems like a tech wizard crossing domains.

That's where your actual value lies. The real flex?

Your *skill stack*—the unique combo of what you know, what you can do, and how you solve problems like a tech wizard crossing domains.

It is not "I code Python."

It's not "I crunch numbers."

It is "I build apps that make users stan and businesses stack cash."

It is "I turn chaotic data into decisions that yeet startups to the moon."

Think about it—the IT world's a neon jungle, moving faster than the Insta trend.

Quick Stat: A 2024 LinkedIn study says 70% of tech jobs now demand cross-functional skills, such as *coding and communication, tech and teamwork, logic, and leadership.*

The ones climbing the ranks are not the coders with the shiniest titles or the longest GitHub streaks. They're the ones who connect the dots: *code with context, tech with teams, logic with leadership.*

They are the T-shaped hustlers who can deep-dive into their craft (the vertical bar) while flexing across domains (the horizontal bar).

In other words, they have a deep expertise in one area (the vertical bar) and a broad understanding of different areas (the horizontal bar), making them versatile and adaptable.

This chapter is your cheat code to becoming that force—a tech chameleon who adapts, learns smart, and builds a career that slaps harder than a viral X thread.

Adaptability is the secret weapon in the tech landscape for the ever-evolving World.

Cilly, a 22-year-old Gen-Z frontend dev who started as a React newbie at a mid-tier startup.

Her title? "Junior Developer."

Her stack? Way spicier.

Sure, she codes pixel-perfect UI, but she also understands user behavior from A/B tests, pitches features in stand-ups, and even dabbles in AWS to deploy her apps.

When her team's PM bailed, Cilly stepped up, syncing designers and backend devs like a Discord mod herding a raid.

Her secret? She didn't just stack *tech* skills—she stacked *context.*

She learned to speak "business" (ROI, user retention) and "people" (empathy, clarity).

Result? A promotion to "Tech Lead" in 18 months, while her "senior" peers were still gatekeeping their Jira tickets.

Now, contrast with Kai, a data analyst who thought his title was his brand. He crunched numbers like a beast but stayed in his Excel bubble.

When his company pivoted to AI-driven insights, Kai's "I'm just an analyst" vibe left him sidelined. He had no cloud skills, storytelling, or cross-team clout.

Quick Stat - *A 2023 McKinsey stat says 60% of IT pros who don't upskill risk obsolescence by 2030. Kai's not doomed, but he's buffering while Cilly streams in 4 K.*

So, what's the play?

This chapter is a blueprint for crafting a skill stack that's future-proof and versatile, and *you.*

We are diving into

Why T-shaped skills are your superpower: Depth in one area (e.g., coding) plus breadth across others (e.g., UX, biz strat) makes you a Swiss Army knife in tech.

How to build a dope, adaptable stack: From picking the right tools (Python, cloud, soft skills) to learning fast via hackathons, Discords, and #BuildInPublic.

Leveling up from "just a dev" to a tech force: Speak the language of PMs, marketers, and C-suites to become the go-to player who runs the game.

Your stack is not just a list of skills; it is your original story.

Take **Lila**, an Alpha cybersecurity intern who hacked her way to clout.

Her title was "Intern," but her stack? Fire.

Sure, she knew Kali Linux, but she also taught herself ethical hacking, wrote blogs on XSS attacks, and charmed her team with clear Jira updates.

Her stack included technical skills, communication skills, and a proactive problem-solving attitude.

Lila's quick audit saved the day when a client's site got pwned. Her reward? A full-time gig at 19.

Quick Stat -*A 2024 Stack Overflow survey says 65% of hiring managers value "problem-solvers who communicate" over "tech-only" coders. Lila's stack wasn't just tools—it was impact.*

Gen Z and Alpha, you are built for this. You grew up modding Minecraft, speedrunning tutorials on YouTube, and chatting in Discord.

You are not alone on this journey.

You are part of a community that's shaping the future of tech.

Quick Stat - *A 2024 Penn study says 75% of you prioritize flexibility and learning in careers. That's your edge—use it. Stop chasing titles that sound cool on LinkedIn. Chase a stack that makes you clutch in any room, whether a sprint planning sesh or a VC pitch.*

This chapter has the hacks: picking skills that resonate with your why, learning without burning out, and flexing your stack so recruiters stand out.

Are you ready to move fast and learn smart?

Let us code your superpower.

Chapter 4

SKILL STACK OVER JOB TITLE

"Code builds the product. Communication builds trust. Business sense builds the future."

– Aalok

You are probably tired of hearing the same old advice. "Get a fancy job title, climb the corporate ladder, and you've made it."

But let's be real: job titles like "Senior Dev" or "Lead Engineer" don't tell the whole story of today's tech world.

Welcome to *Skill Stack Over Job Title*, where we're flipping the script and showing you how to build a killer skill stack that screams "I'm a tech rockstar" louder than any LinkedIn badge ever could.

Because in 2025 and beyond, it's not about what your title says— it's about what you can *do*.

Think about it, the tech game is moving faster than a viral YouTube sound.

Companies are not just hiring for titles anymore—they want skills that solve real problems.

Quick Stat - *A 2024 Stack Overflow survey found that 78% of hiring managers prioritize a candidate's skill set over their job history. That means* *your ability to code, automate, or communicate can outshine a "Manager" label any day.*

For Gen Z and Alpha, this is your superpower. You're already digital natives, remixing and adapting like pros.

Whether freelancing on Fiverr, building a SaaS as an indie hacker, or learning APIs on YouTube, your skills are your currency.

This chapter will show you how to stack 'em up, flex 'em loud, and let your work do the talking—because a stacked skill set is the ultimate glow-up.

From DBA to Infra Lead: My Paris Adventure

Yo, Gen Z and Alpha, buckle up again for a wild ride from my Hewlett-Packard days that'll make you laugh, cringe, and maybe rethink that "just stick to your job title" vibe.

I'm a Senior Oracle DBA, and three months into my gig at HP in India, I feel like I've cracked the IT code.

Then, boom—my team's shipped off to Paris for my first onsite assignment.

Paris! The Eiffel Tower! Croissants! I'm hyped, imagining myself sipping espresso by the Seine.

My Parisian glow-up was less *Emily in Paris* and more Me *in Panic Mode*.

We land in Paris in August at 8 p.m., but it's bright like a 5 p.m. Insta filter.

My squad consists of nine tech wizards: Siebel pros, Java coders, XML nerds, a project manager, testers, you name it—hits the hotel restaurant, chows down, and crashes.

I open my room's window at 9 p.m., and the Eiffel Tower lights up like it's throwing me a personal welcome party.

I'm shook, thinking, "Paris, you get me." Hold that thought, fam, because day one of our transition project yeeted my confidence into the Seine.

At the first meeting, I'm suited and ready to flex my Oracle 8i and 9i certifications.

The client, Mr. Julien, a French tech boss with a vibe that says Bonjour, 'I've seen it all," hits me with a curveball - "Aalok, you're handling Siebel infrastructure and integrations for all 13 tech stacks, and we are all transitioning over six months to you, right?" I freeze.

Siebel? Infra? *Thirteen* techs?

I glance at my project manager, Sanjay, who's giving me the "bro, you're on your own" eyes.

Before I can recover, Julien drops another, "You're solid on Oracle DB, yes?

We've struggled to find the right DBA." I blurt, "Certified in 8i and 9i!" Julien smiles, Sanjay exhales, and I think, "Cool, I'm safe."

But I am not feeling *safe.*

Post-meeting, I cornered Sanjay and said, "Yo, you said this was a DBA gig—migrate databases."

Chill vibes. Now I'm supposed to orchestrate 13 techs, write docs, test in Dev and QA, and hand off to the global team every quarter?

What's good?" Sanjay's face screams regret.

"Aalok, my bad. During due diligence, we missed the infra lead role.

You're the closest we've got to infra skills, so you're it.

Now sending you back to India's not an option—it'll tank my job.

"I'm fuming, but my gut's like, "You're in Paris, bro. You can't just rage-quit."

Then I asked for 24 hours to think. Back in my room, I Googled "Siebel integrations" like a noob, realizing I was in over my head.

But quitting? Not my brand.

I rolled up to Sanjay the next day with a plan, channeling my inner *Shark Tank* pitch.

"I'm in, but here's the deal: hook me up with a Siebel expert who knows file and parameter-level integrations for all 13 techs, and I need full team support.

Oh, and you're crowning me Infra Lead—client, team, everyone."

Sanjay's eyes widen at "Infra Lead," but he's desperate and agrees.

At the next meeting, he announces, "Aalok's our stop-gap Infra Lead.

Give him your full support."

The team—senior tech gods with egos bigger than the Arc de Triomphe—side-eyes me like.

"This DBA's out here cosplaying a lead?" I'm sweating, but my gut's screaming, "Mera time aayega!" (My time's coming, fam.)

Here's where the real hustle kicked in.

Leading a team of tech titans as a non-infra-DBA was like modding a game you've never played.

My strategy?

Keep it 100, no ego, all vibes.

These are the hacks that turned my Parisian panic into a leadership glow-up.

Respect Over Rivalry: My team was salty—senior coders didn't vibe with a DBA leading. I stayed chill, never clapping back in the shade.

Respect was my currency, and it earned me trust.

Quick Stat - *A 2024 Harvard study says 70% of tech leads win teams over with empathy, not tech flexes. Facts.*

Learn the Handshake, Not the Code: I did not try to outcode the Java or XML pros. Instead, I mastered how the 13 techs "talked" at the file and parameter level—think of it as learning the API of their vibes. Google, coffee, and late-night docs were my senseis.

Context Is Clutch: I dug into the *business* side of each tech. If the "Data Framework XML App" crashed at 8 a.m., I knew which downstream app would tank by 10 a.m. and how it'd hit the client's bottom line.

Clients started calling *me* during incidents, not the PM, because I spoke "impact," not just "DBA."

Quick Stat: A 2023 McKinsey study says that 65% of IT pros who understand the business context are *fast-tracked to leadership.*

By month six, I was not just a DBA—I was an *Integration Infra Lead DBA* who glued 13 techs together and kept the client smiling.

My skill stack—Oracle, integration basics, people skills, and business savvy—outshone my title.

The team? They went from side-eyes to "Aalok's clutch.

"Sanjay? Safe. Me?

Leveled up, ready for bigger quests.

And the outcome was that we got the "*Best Infra Transition Award.*"

Don't chase titles—build your toolbox. Because when the tech tide turns, skills float - *Titles sink.*

Lessons That Slap for Gen Z & Alpha

Adapt or Get 404'd: I had zero infra skills but leaned into the chaos.

Quick Stat - *A 2024 LinkedIn stat says 68% of young IT pros land gigs by pivoting fast. Say "yes" to scary roles, then Google like your career depends on it.*

Respect Wins Wars: Ego's a trap. Stay humble, and even salty seniors will stan. Your vibe's your real stack.

Context > Code: Knowing *why* tech matters (e.g., business impact) makes you the MVP. Learn to speak "client," not just "commit."

Stack Over Title: My DBA certs got me in the room, but my skill stack—tech, people, context—kept me there. Build yours, flex it.

Action Steps to Hustle Smart

#AdaptVibes Challenge: *Pick one skill outside your role (e.g., cloud basics for coders). Spend 30 minutes daily on YouTube tutorials for a week. Post progress on X with #DigitalHustle.*

Context Quest: *At work, ask your PM, "How does my task impact the client?" Journal the answer to level up your business game.*

Respect Flex: *DM a senior colleague on Slack: "I loved your [task]. Do you have any tips for a newbie?" Build bridges, not beef.*

Remember: *Your Titles are just Wi-Fi bars, but your skill stack is the Signal that keeps you connected, Clutched, and coding the future like a 2030 Boss.*

Your value is no longer tied to a fixed title in today's fast-moving tech environments. Titles are outdated within months, but skill stacks evolve with you.

A skill stack is your combination of hard and soft skills—unique, adaptable, and more potent than any single certification.

Quick Stat: *According to the World Economic Forum (2023), the most in-demand tech roles now require hybrid competencies—not just technical mastery but also communication, collaboration, and commercial thinking.*

Let me introduce T-Shaped Skills- Why Does It Matter in IT Careers?

The Title Trap.

I once met a guy whose email signature was longer than his resume.

"Rahul Sharma, Lead Principal Chief Cloud Orchestrator, Digital Strategy Division – Asia-Pacific & Emerging Markets, Level 7"

He had one job: to restart stuck containers.

Now, I'm not here to roast Rahul (okay, maybe just a light toasting), but to point out how often we get obsessed with titles in tech.

"Full Stack Ninja," "DevOps Evangelist,"

"AI Whisperer"—it's an arms race of adjectives.

But behind all the glittering job names, there's a deeper question?

Can you get stuff done?

When the production server catches fire, are you running toward it or updating your LinkedIn headline?

This chapter is your call to stop playing title-chess and start stacking fundamental, adaptable skills that keep you future-proof, employable, and respected in any room.

The T-Shaped Talent (Imagine the letter T)

- The vertical line (|) indicates deep expertise in one area, such as database engineering, backend dev, cybersecurity, etc. To become an expert in this tech skill, you must go to levels 3 and 4.

- The horizontal bar (—) is broad knowledge across other relevant areas, like version control, APIs, cloud basics, or soft skills like client communication and project management. You need to know several skills, but going deeper may not be necessary. You need to under the relevance of the tech where it is used, why, and the business context as appropriate.

Real Talk: What T-Shaped Looks Like at Work

Let me take you behind the scenes.

At TechM days, we had a junior developer from the app side, Amit, who was a Java wizard.

Like, "talks to the JVM in his sleep" level.

But hand him a git conflict, and he'd stare like it was a riddle from The Da Vinci Code.

Now compare that to Sneha, a mid-level dev. She wasn't the best at Java, but she could debug a Jenkins job, talk to clients, help QA, or jump into shell scripts without panic.

Guess who got the promotion?

Yep, the one who didn't just go deep, but also wide.

WHY THIS MODEL WORKS: 5 REASONS

The Tech World Changes Faster Than Chai Cools Down

- JavaScript today, Rust tomorrow. Oracle now, Postgres later. The only way to survive is to adapt.

- T-shaped folks adapt faster—they don't panic when change hits. They pivot.

Collaboration Demands a Shared Vocabulary

- You don't need to master design, but understanding UX lingo helps you work with UI folks.

- Devs who understand testing or can talk like a PM get things done faster—and better.

You Become the Go-To Person

- Teams love people who can fill gaps when others are stuck.

- Someone is out sick, and a script is failing in production?

- T-shaped, you jump in, save the day, and earn reputation points.

Breadth = Leadership Potential

- Senior roles need vision. Vision needs cross-functional understanding.

- Every significant tech lead I know is at least T-shaped, often even π-shaped (two deep skills!).

You Avoid the "One-Trick Pony" Trap

- If all you know is Flash animation, well, sorry.

- Specialization without versatility is a career risk in IT.

Stat Zone: Don't Just Take My Word for It (Quick Stat)

- *LinkedIn's Future of Skills Report (2023) says versatility and cross-functional knowledge are now top priorities for hiring managers in tech roles.*

- *McKinsey research found that T-shaped teams outperform siloed teams by 25% in delivery speed and 35% in cross-functional satisfaction.*

- *Google's hiring philosophy values "learning ability" over "current expertise"—a trait naturally found in T-shaped professionals.*

But Wait—Isn't Depth Still Important?

Absolutely. You can't be all frosting and no cake.

- Your depth is what gives you confidence.

- Your breadth is what gives you options.

If you only skim everything, you become a "Jack of all trades, master of none."

But with T-shaped growth, you pick a lane to master, while keeping your head up and curious.

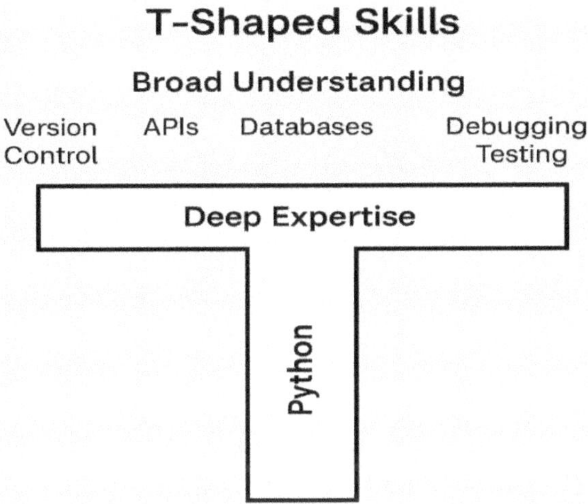

A PRACTICAL GUIDE TO BUILDING YOUR SKILL STACK

Step one: Identify Your Vertical

- What's your strongest area today? Backend? DevOps? AI? UI?

- Go deeper. Find the pain points. Learn the frameworks.

- Contribute to open source. Get certified.

Step two: Build Horizontal Awareness

- Pick 2–3 adjacent skill areas. For backend devs, that could be:

  - Git workflows

  - Basic frontend debugging

  - CI/CD pipelines

- Cloud services (AWS/GCP)
- Spend 20% of your learning time there.

Step three: Use the 70-20-10 Rule

- 70%: Do your core job and deepen skills
- 20%: Explore adjacent topics that helps team constructive collaboration
- 10%: Experiment or play with wild cards—like public speaking or writing blog posts

Step four: Talk to Real People

- Join team retros. Volunteer for cross-team demos.
- Don't shyly say, "I don't know—but I want to learn."
- Knowledge spreads fastest through conversation.

Remember - *"In tech, depth makes you credible. Breadth makes you promotable, and when in doubt, learn just enough to ask intelligent questions.*

My Printer & SCO Unix Moment

Remember my story in week two of my IBM job? I volunteered to migrate an Informix database from SCO Unix to Windows 2000, without knowing what Informix even was.)

It was not bravery. It was curiosity + mild panic + some Google-fu.

I used my Oracle DB knowledge (depth) and mapped it against Informix docs (breadth).

I was not the best DBA, but I knew enough to figure out what needed to be done, stitch tools together, and get it working.

Did I break the office printer in the process? Yes.

Did I learn how to become adaptable? Also Yes.

Move self from T to π to Comb-shaped?

Some people grow two depths—maybe frontend and backend, or DevOps and security. That's π-shaped.

Even better?

Comb-shaped—breadth across many things with moderate depth in a few.

But don't stress about that yet.

Just build your T.

But listen with care. OK, Be the Architect, not the Actor.

Titles come and go. Teams restructure. Tools evolve.

But a strong skill stack means you're never locked out of opportunity.

"Instead of waiting for someone to hand you a better title—build a better toolbox."

So, when your next chance comes—a project, a promotion, or a pivot—you are not asking.

"Do I have the title?" You're saying, "Let me show you what I can do."

Because in the tech world, **the best careers are not handed out— they're engineered.**

CROSS-FUNCTIONAL FLUENCY - HOW TO BUILD?

We are in the Age of the Unicorns

In today's tech world, job titles lie. That guy labeled "Frontend Developer" might be debugging API calls.

The "Marketing Associate" is running SQL queries. The "Data Analyst" is giving business strategy inputs in C-level meetings. The game has changed.

Welcome to the era where adaptability isn't optional—it's your default operating system.

In this chapter, we also unpack how building fluency across three critical domains—coding, *Communication, and Business Thinking*—gives you an unfair advantage in a career that refuses to stay in one lane.

WHY CROSS-FUNCTIONAL FLUENCY?

Let's start with the facts (Quick Stat)

- *According to McKinsey (2023), 43% of high-growth companies prioritize hiring multi-skilled employees over specialists.*

- *LinkedIn's 2024 Talent Trends revealed that "adaptability" and "collaboration across functions" are among the top five soft skills in demand.*

- *Harvard Business Review notes that "the most valuable employees can translate technical complexity into business outcomes."*

So, the question is no longer **"What's your role?"** The real question is:

"Can you speak multiple professional languages?"

The Stack That Pays: Code + Talk + Think

If your skills were an app stack, the magic formula would look like this:

- Tech IQ (Code): Can you build or understand systems?
- People IQ (Communication): Can you express clearly, listen better, and pitch smart?
- Business IQ (Context): Do you know *why* your code or feature matters to the customer or bottom line?

This trifecta makes you a "Techno Translator"—someone who bridges gaps, builds credibility quickly, and grows quickly.

A Story from the Trenches: The PM Who Didn't Code (but Still Shipped Big)

Coding + Communication + Business

In my early career, I encountered a Project Manager who had never written much of the production code.

On paper, she (Priya) should've struggled in our hardcore dev-led team, but she was *an adaptable person.*

She'd sit in dev stand-ups, understand dependencies, and take notes in a GSheet that made sense to both backend and business teams.

She didn't just communicate—she translated. She *asked questions* that made senior engineers rethink architecture decisions.

And she often brought insights from customer support data that the engineering team had ignored.

The result? Features that didn't just work, they *won.* That's cross-functional fluency in action.

Coding - Don't Just Learn, Understand What to Automate

Coding is not just syntax. It's systems thinking. If you're from a non-tech background, start with this rule: Don't chase becoming a coding genius.

Focus on becoming code-literate

- Know how APIs talk.
- Understand what the frontend and backend handshake looks like.
- Learn how data flows.

Real-World Use Case

A marketing exec I mentored learned just enough Python to automate repetitive Excel reports. In 3 months, he saved 6 hours weekly and was promoted for "efficiency improvements."

Remember - *You don't need to become a developer. But you do need to think like one.*

Communication - Code is Hard, Explaining It Is Harder

You can be the most intelligent person in the room. But that matters if you can explain your solution on a whiteboard.

Communication = Compression + Clarity

Whether you are pitching to a client, writing documentation, or updating your manager:

- Speak their language.
- Drop the jargon.
- Use analogies. (Think: "Our API is like a vending machine...")

Real-Life Win

An engineer used Lego bricks in a client demo to explain modular microservices. The client signed a six-figure contract in that meeting.

Remember—your *value increases with your vocabulary. Learn to tell your story, or someone else will define your narrative.*

Business - It's Not Just Code. It's Code With Purpose

Every line of code affects a metric: retention, cost, and user satisfaction. And that's where *Business IQ* comes in.

Ask yourself:

- Who is using this?

- What problem am I solving?
- How does this feature connect to revenue or cost?

Quick Stat - *According to Forrester (2023), teams with product awareness and business acumen deliver 37% faster and see 21% fewer post-launch rollbacks.*

Use Case - A dev team I worked with once spent weeks optimizing a backend storage backup job query. The ops team said it reduced infra cost notionally by $500/month.

When did they work on onboarding UI friction instead? The activation rate jumped by 11%, which mattered more.

Ship fast" is fine, but ship *smart* wins. Business fluency keeps you relevant.

MICRO-MASTERY

How to Build Cross-Functional Fluency (Without Burning Out)

Pick One New Domain Every Quarter

- Q1: Take a course on persuasive writing
- Q2: Learn basic SQL
- Q3: Read "The Lean Startup."
- Q4: Join a cross-functional project

Shadow Roles for a Day

Ask a Product Manager or Sales teammate if you can sit in on a call or review. You'll learn more than any certification can offer.

Teach to Learn: Start a blog or internal newsletter explaining tech to non-techies or vice versa.

Build a Side Project with a Friend from Another Domain

Developer + designer = product

Salesperson + coder = prototype

Ops + dev = automation

The goal is not to be everything. The goal is to *collaborate* as if you understand everything.

Modern Job Market: The New Talent Stack

The top recruiters today are not just looking for degrees or titles. They want:

- *A frontend dev who understands conversion rates.*
- *A data analyst who can present findings in a story.*
- *A support engineer who spots trends and pitches improvements.*

LinkedIn CEO Ryan Roslansky said, *"The most valuable career skill? Learnability—the ability to learn, unlearn, and relearn at speed."*

And remember,

You are not a job title. You are a skills cocktail. Stir well. Serve fresh.

Adaptability is not a Buzzword. It is a Career Strategy.

Let's face it, job roles are evolving faster than college curricula.

The only constant is change, and your ability to dance with it.

So, whether you are a coder who starts presenting client demos or a business analyst who learns to script in Python, every step toward cross-functional fluency is a step toward career freedom.

In the future of work, your edge won't be how deep you are in one thing—it'll be how wide your bridge connects the dots.

CONCLUSION

Your edge is in the Bridge. We live in the Age of the Unicorns—not the mythical creatures, but the modern professionals who blend logic with empathy, code with conversation, and execution with strategy.

In this chapter, you've seen why building fluency across Coding, Communication, and Business isn't a luxury—it's a survival skill.

This trifecta gives you *range*, your insurance policy against a job market that refuses to sit still.

"Titles Are Getting Blurrier. Skills Are Getting Sharper."

Let's face it. In today's tech world, job titles lie.

A "Frontend Dev" might be configuring APIs.

A "Marketing Analyst" might be writing Python scripts.

A "Support Engineer" might be influencing roadmap priorities.

The world is no longer siloed—and neither should you be.

The question is no longer *"What do you do?"*

"What problems can you solve—and in how many languages?"

Cross-functional fluency is about becoming the person who connects the dots—

The person who understands the *code*, explains the *why*, and aligns it with the *business goal*.

These professionals don't just survive transitions—they lead them.

Code Alone Isn't Enough

We are not saying you must become a full-stack genius.

But you do need to be code-*literate*.

Understand how the systems work. Know what an API does.

Learn enough automation to save time and unlock ideas.

Because here's the truth, business problems don't come in JavaScript. They come in chaos. And your job is to organize that chaos—sometimes with a script, a slide, and a strategy.

Communicating Like a Creator

You could be the most innovative technologist in the room, but your brilliance gets lost if you cannot explain your work in simple, human words.

Compression and clarity are more important than charisma.

Whether you are demoing a feature or writing a stakeholder update, think like a storyteller.

Use metaphors.

Use empathy.

Use the language your audience speaks.

Because at the end of the day, ideas don't win.

Ideas that land.

Business Sense Is Your Compass

Every feature you build, tool you choose, and ticket you close adds up to a metric that matters: revenue, retention, experience, and efficiency.

So, do not write code just for elegance.

Write it for *impact*.

Understand what the customer is struggling with.

Ask how your work affects the business model.

Business fluency isn't about wearing a suit. It's about making your tech efforts *matter*.

You Don't Master Everything—Grow Outside Your Lane

Here's your practical path forward

- *Each quarter, explore one domain outside your comfort zone.*
- *Shadow a colleague from another department.*

- *Teach what you know. Please write a blog, make a Loom video, or explain it to a friend.*

- *Join a side project with someone who speaks a different "professional language."*

This is how you build fluency without burning out.

Remember- *The goal is not to become everything. The goal is to collaborate as if you understand everything.*

The New Talent Stack - The world's top recruiters aren't chasing perfect résumés. They are chasing people who move fluidly across domains:

- *A designer who understands conversion.*

- *A developer who reads feedback like a product owner.*

- *A data analyst who can pitch insights like a marketer.*

In this new era, learnability beats legacy.

Whether you're an introvert coder who starts hosting client demos or a sales pro who learns to build chatbots, every cross-functional step you take pushes you one level closer to career freedom.

So build your bridge. One domain at a time.

And when the world asks, "What do you do?"—smile and say: "Whatever the problem needs."

Remember: *"In the future of work, your edge won't be how deep you are in one thing—it will be how wide your bridge connects the dots."*

Action Vibe-Check

- **Stack Audit:** *List three skills you have (e.g., Python, Figma) and one you want (e.g., cloud). Google a free course to start this week.*

- **#StackSlaps Post:** *Share your dream stack on X: "Coding + UX + pitching = my IT superpower. What's yours? #DigitalHustle."*

- **Squad Sync:** *DM a tech bro on LinkedIn: "Yo, how'd you add [skill] to your stack?" Their reply might spark your next move.*

Chapter 5

STAY LEARNING OR STAY STUCK

"Your future progress won't depend on how fast you write code, but how well you connect the code to resolve customer business problems."

– Aalok

You are probably juggling a million tabs—coding on GitHub, scrolling X for the latest AI trends, or watching a YouTube crash course on cloud platforms.

But here's the real question - Are you *learning* through it all, or just stuck in the same loop?

Welcome to *Stay Learning or Stay Stuck*, where we're diving into the ultimate tech truth—you have gotta keep learning, or you will get left behind faster than a dead meme.

For digital natives like you, staying curious is not just a flex but your ticket to thriving in an always-updating world.

Quick Stat - *The tech game doesn't chill. A 2024 Gartner report says 65% of tech skills have a shelf life of less than three years, meaning what you know today might be obsolete by 2028.*

Gen Z and Alpha, you are already wired for this. You have grown up remixing playlists and adapting to new apps overnight.

This chapter will show you how to apply that energy to tech—stacking skills, staying curious, and never getting stuck. Because in 2025 and beyond, learning is not optional—it is your need of the hour.

Let's keep your tech journey on fire!

During my US Workdays, I came across - The Scroll Trap!

In the neon-lit sprawl of New Avalon, 17-year-old Celestia Moon ('C') is a legend in her DMs.

Her phone was her scepter, her YouTube feed her kingdom.

She was the queen of clout in high school with many followers and a knack for viral dance vids.

But IRL? Celestia was coasting.

School was a vibe she barely tolerated, and her grades were a chaotic mood board of Cs and Ds.

"Why grind on algebra when I'm already popping off online?

"She'd say, tossing her lavender streaked hair.

Her mantra: *Slay now, stress later.*

Celestia's best friend, Kai, was the epitome of a tech nerd. With a 4.0 GPA and a side hustle coding apps, he was the polar opposite of Celestia.

Kai's room was a shrine to DIY Arduino projects and dog-eared sci-fi novels. He dragged Celestia to the coding club, but she laughed it off.

"Bro, I'm not about that keyboard warrior life. I'm out here *living.*"

Kai shook his head, muttering, "You're one algorithm change away from being irrelevant, C."

One sweaty afternoon, Celestia was sprawled on her bed, doomscrolling through X, when a notification pinged.

It was a DM from @QuantumHustle, some rando with a galaxy-themed PFP.

The message read: *Want to level up IRL? Meet me at Neon Arcade at 7 PM. Bring your A-game or stay basic.*

Celestia snorted. "Sounds like a scam, but I'm bored."

She threw on her favorite cropped hoodie, grabbed her vape, and headed out, ready to clap back at whoever this cryptic weirdo was.

The Neon Arcade was a retro glow-up, all flickering CRTs and claw machines.

Celestia spotted a figure in a black bomber jacket, hood up, leaning against a Street Fighter cabinet.

"Yo, QuantumHustle?" she called, popping her gum.

The figure turned, revealing a girl about Celestia's age with electric blue braids and a smirk sharper than a fresh manicure. "Call me Nova," she said.

"You, Celestia Moon? The YouTuber "princess" *who thinks she's got life hacked?*"

Celestia bristled. "I'm out here thriving, fam. *What's your deal?*"

Nova's eyes glinted.

"My deal? I'm a recruiter for Nexus, a crew that turns wannabes into winners.

But you? You are stuck in the scroll trap, chasing likes while the world passes you.

Bet you can't even code a 'Hello World' script."

Celestia laughed, but it came out shaky. "I don't need to code. I'm building my brand."

"Brands crash, Celestia. Skills stack." Nova slid a sleek tablet across the arcade table.

It displayed a challenge: Hack the arcade's leaderboard in 24 hours. There was no phone and no followers, just your brain. Win, and the Nexus trains you to run the game. Lose, and stay a spectator.

Celestia's stomach flipped. "This is giving major sketch vibes. *What's the catch?*"

"No catch," Nova said. "Just a choice: stay learning or stay stuck." She leaned in, voice low. "Clock's ticking, queen. *What's it gonna be?*"

It was a wake-up call for Celestia Moon.

She took the tablet, not to prove anything to Nova but herself.

Back home, she stared at the screen displaying a Python and network protocols tutorial.

"This is straight-up torture," she groaned, tossing the tablet onto her bed.

But Nova's words echoed: *Stay a spectator.*

Celestia was not about to let some cyberpunk wannabe call her out like that. She cracked her knuckles and dove in, ready to prove that she was more than a spectator.

The first few hours were a disaster. Python syntax was like trying to decipher alien hieroglyphs.

Celestia's confidence tanked as error messages piled up.

She almost deleted the tablet from her window, but remembered Kai. If anyone could help her avoid this, it was him.

She FaceTimed Kai, who was mid-solder on some robot arm project. "C, you look like you just got rationed by life," he said, pushing up his glasses.

Celestia spilled tea about Nova and the Nexus challenge. Kai's eyes lit up.

"Bruh, this is legit! You're hacking an arcade leaderboard?

That's next-level. I'm in."

Kai became Celestia's Yoda, breaking down Python like a YouTuber dance routine.

"Think of code as choreography," he said. "Each line's a step.

Mess up the order, you faceplant." By midnight, Celestia had a shaky script to ping the arcade's network.

By 3 AM, she and Kai were deep in a Discord call, debugging like their lives depended on it.

Celestia's brain was fried, but she felt alive for the first time in forever, not because of likes or clout but because of building something real.

The next evening, Celestia and Kai snuck into the arcade after hours, using a backdoor Kai had scoped out.

Celestia's script ran on the tablet, probing the leaderboard's ancient server. Her heart raced as the terminal spat out: *Access granted.*

They were in. Celestia tweaked the leaderboard, planting her initials—ZNG—at the top of every game. The screen flashed with a new message: *Challenge complete. Nexus awaits.*

Celestia fist-bumped Kai, adrenaline pumping.

"We did that, fam! I'm Anonymous now."

Kai grinned. "You're a noob with potential. Don't get it twisted."

The next night, Celestia Moon met Nova at an abandoned warehouse that became a cyberpunk HQ.

Neon signs buzzed, and holographic displays floated above workstations where teens typed furiously.

"Welcome to the Nexus," Nova said. "This is where we train the next gen to run the world, not just react to it."

Celestia's jaw dropped.

"This gives Black Mirror vibes, but I'm here for it."

Nova introduced Celestia to the crew: Lila, a graphic designer who coded VR worlds; Mateo, a former dropout turned AI whisperer; and Priya, a biohacker who grows glowing plants.

They were all Celestia's age, but their skills were God-tier.

"These kids didn't wait for permission," Nova said.

"They learned, built, and hustled. You in or what?"

Celestia nodded, but doubt crept in. "I barely survived that arcade hack. What if I can't keep up?"

Nova smirked. "Then you'll learn, or you'll crash. No one's carrying you here."

The Nexus training was brutal.

Celestia spent weeks learning to code, design circuits, and even dabble in machine learning. Her phone gathered dust as she traded likes for logic.

She wanted to rage-quit some nights, especially when her neural network model failed for the 50th time.

But Kai's voice echoed in her head: *Mess up the order, you faceplant.* She kept grinding.

One day, Priya caught Celestia staring at her glowing plants.

"Wanna know how I made these?" Priya asked.

Celestia shrugged, expecting a lecture, but Priya handed her a CRISPR kit. "Learn by doing, not watching."

Celestia spent the next week geeking over gene editing, her YouTube muscle memory replaced by pipette precision.

She started to see the world differently—not as a stage for clout, but as a puzzle to solve.

Three months into The Big Hack, Nova dropped a bombshell. Nexus had a final test: a city-wide hackathon to redesign New Avalon's public transit system.

The prize? A chance to pitch to the mayor and score funding for their startup.

The catch? They'd compete against corporate-backed teams with Ivy League coders and unlimited budgets.

Celestia's team—her, Kai, Priya, and Mateo—called themselves the Neon Underdogs.

Their plan was ambitious: an AI-driven transit app that optimized routes in real-time, powered by crowdsourced data and solar-powered sensors.

Celestia led the UI, channeling her YouTube Channel aesthetic into a sleek, Gen Z-friendly design.

Kai handled the AI, Priya engineered the sensors, and Mateo secured the backend.

The hackathon was a 48-hour blur of Red Bull, bugs, and banter. Celestia's team hit a wall when their AI kept spitting out garbage routes.

"This is a total L," Celestia groaned, rubbing her eyes.

Half-dead from caffeine, Kai snapped, "Stop whining and debug, 'C.' We're not here to vibe; we're here to win."

Celestia took a deep breath, remembering Nova's words: *Skills stack.* She dove into the code, line by line, until she spotted the issue—a misconfigured data pipeline. She fixed it, and the AI roared to life, mapping routes smoother than a viral transition.

The team cheered, and Celestia felt a rush no follower count could match.

On demo day, the Neon Underdogs faced teams in suits who oozed privilege. Celestia's nerves were glitching, but she channeled her inner influence, delivering a fiery pitch that could've trended on X.

Their app wowed the judges, blending practicality with a vibe that screamed *"This is for us, by us."* When the mayor announced the winners, the Neon Underdogs took first place.

The crowd erupted, and Celestia's team mobbed each other, screaming, "We popped off!" Nova watched from the sidelines, nodding.

"Not bad, Celestia. You're learning."

The Glow-Up: A year later, Celestia was not just a YouTube relic but a Nexus legend.

The Neon Underdogs' app, *TransitGlow*, was live, saving New Avalon commuters hours daily.

Celestia still posted vids, but now they were about coding hacks and biohacking tutorials, racking up views from kids who saw her as proof you could slay *and* learn.

She and Kai planned a startup to teach coding through gaming, with Priya and Mateo on board.

Celestia grades? Straight like her vibe? Was Unstoppable. She'd traded the scrolled-up trap for a life of building, learning, and flexing skills that no algorithm could nerf. One night, chilling at the arcade with Nova, Celestia grinned.

"Bet you thought I'd flop. Nova Smile was converted into a big laugh. "I knew you had it in you. You just needed a wake-up call. So, what's next?"

Celestia's eyes sparkled. "World domination, duh. But first, I'm coding a claw machine hack to win Kai a plushie."

The epilogue Moral of the Celestia Moon story is not just a glow-up montage—it's a wake-up call.

The world does not care about your follower count; it rewards those who keep learning, building, and pushing. Clout is a sugar rush, but skills are a feast.

So, pick your path: *Stay learning or stay stuck.*

Remember—you can't Yeet your way to success, fam—grind, grow, and glow, or get left alone *by life*.

WHY ARE CERTIFICATIONS, REAL-WORLD PROJECTS & THE 70/20/10 RULE CRITICAL?

Lifelong Learning in Tech is the Harsh Truth About Tech Careers:

"In tech, if you're not learning, you're not standing still—you're sliding backward." The shelf-life of a tech skill is shrinking.

Quick Stat -*According to a report by LinkedIn Learning, the average skill becomes obsolete in just 2.5 years.*

That's shorter than a Netflix subscription cycle. If you're waiting for a job title to make you feel secure, the bad news is that job titles are lagging indicators.

Learning is the only way to lead.

We do not live in a world of "learn once, work forever" anymore.

We live in a world of "learn always or become irrelevant."

Do not feel overwhelmed by reading this harsh truth.

Remember what we learned in the Mindset chapter.

Your approach and attitude determine whether you make it Harsh or Entertaining.

WHY LIFELONG LEARNING ISN'T OPTIONAL ANYMORE

Let's lay down the reality (Quick Stat)

- *Gartner* reports that 58% of the workforce will require new skills to do their jobs effectively.
- *The World Economic Forum* predicts 44% of workers' core skills will change in the next 5 years.
- In a McKinsey survey, 87% of executives said they're already experiencing skill gaps or expect them shortly.

Whether a fresher or a fifth-year senior, tech doesn't care how long you've been around.

It cares how fast you can adapt. Lifelong learning isn't a buzzword. It's your career insurance.

Remember - *Tech doesn't reward the most experienced. It rewards the most adaptable.*

Ever heard of the 70/20/10 rule?- Microlearning Learning that Sticks:

It's a proven adult learning framework that applies beautifully to tech careers.

- **70% Learning by Doing** - Build things. Break things. Fix them. Real learning happens *while shipping*, not studying.

- Projects teach you context, edge cases, and creative problem-solving.

- **20% Learning from Others** - Mentors, feedback, peer code reviews, team retrospectives—this is where wisdom meets practice.

- **10% Structured Learning** - Courses, certifications, webinars, books—great for foundations and theory.

Remember - *You can't learn swimming from PowerPoint. You've got to go into the pool.*

Quick Case Study - The Dev Who Skipped the Degree

Take Prashant, a self-taught Oracle DBA and SQL Developer. He did not go to college after 12th grade. He spent 6 months on micro-courses, built a portfolio of 2 Oracle Databases in real-world projects, got feedback in online communities, and landed a Job.

He followed the 70/20/10 rule *without even knowing it.*

Microlearning—Small Bytes, Big Wins

Attention spans are short, and life is busy.

Enter **microlearning**—*short, focused bursts of learning that fit into your daily routine.*

Instead of a 3-hour weekend course, do this

- 10 minutes of Git command practice on your lunch break.

- 1 DevOps YouTube explainer before bed.

- Solve 1 LeetCode problem each morning.

Apps like Mimo, Sololearn, Enki, and ByteByteGo make tech skills bite-sized and digestible. You can master one concept a day and stay ahead—without burning out.

Remember - *Learning is a habit, not an event.*

Let's do some Quick Stat Check

- *According to the Journal of Applied Psychology, microlearning improves focus and retention by **80%**.*

- *Learners are **50% more likely** to complete bite-sized content than full-length courses (Talent LMS).*

Most Critical Certifications—Proof of Progress

Yes, skills matter more than certs. But don't underestimate what certifications *signal*, especially when breaking into a new domain or job level.

Few Top Gen-AI / Tech Certifications for 2025

- Google Cloud Gen AI Engineering
- NVIDIA Deep Learning Institute
- IBM AI Engineering
- Microsoft Azure AI Fundamentals
- Coursera's Prompt Engineering by Vanderbilt University
- AWS Certified Machine Learning – Specialty

Certs are not your end goal—they are your conversation starter

They get your resume on the table. Your project portfolio and communication keep it there.

Remember - *Be watchful of the certification trend every six months.*

⚠ **Warning:** *Don't stack certs like Pokémon cards. Stack them like stepping stones.*

Real-World Projects—Your Ultimate Classroom

No course will teach you what a broken deployment at 2 AM does.

No tutorial prepares you for misaligned expectations with a product owner.

Want to learn fast?

- Contribute to open source.
- Join a hackathon.
- Build a no-code MVP (Minimal Viable Product) with a friend.
- Help a local business automate reports.
- Volunteer as a tech mentor in a student group.
- Create your own light-minded (Master Mind Tech group)

Real-world projects teach the messy, unpredictable, deeply human side of tech.

See, "You learn more from a failed side project than a perfect tutorial."

Remember - *"True experience is not just about time served—it is about how many times you have failed, learned, and bounced back stronger. That is why people say you either have success or experience. Because failure is just an event, success is a journey—it is the classroom where you earn it."*

Reflect, Adapt, and Use Every Setback to Shape a Better Tomorrow.

Create Your Own Learning Operating System - Learning MAP

Do not just learn reactively. Learn with INTENT. Here's a simple framework:

Step 1: Pick a domain (e.g., "Cloud", "Prompt Engineering", "APIs")

Step 2: Identify ONE certification + ONE mentor + ONE project idea

Step 3: Apply the 70/20/10 rule for the next 90 days

Step 4: Reflect → Document → Teach someone else

Note the Mini habit: *Every Sunday, ask yourself: What did I learn this week, and where did I apply it?*

Unlearn to Relearn—The Career Superpower

Sometimes, the most challenging part of learning is *unlearning*.

Unlearning your ego. Unlearning "how it's always been done."

Unlearning the idea that tech mastery is about memorizing syntax.

The best learners aren't know-it-alls. They're just change-ready.

Remember - *In tech, the skill that pays the most isn't coding—it's evolving.*

The key takeaway - "In a world that's changing fast, learning is your hustle coin."

You do not need a degree from MIT.

But you need:

- A curious mind,
- A consistent schedule,
- And a compass that says: *"Stay learning or stay stuck."*
- Keep in mind to make tomorrow better than today.

Because in this world of AI, automation, and acceleration, the job market doesn't care what you once knew. It cares what you're learning right now.

So, repeat this simple affirmation three times. I am serious.

Say it out loud. Later, take a sticky note and write it on it.

Please keep it in front of your desk, where you can read or keep it in front of you.

"I will learn fast. I will apply faster. I will never stop learning."

"I will learn fast. I will apply faster. I will never stop learning."

"I will learn fast. I will apply faster. I will never stop learning."

CONCLUSION

Let's hit pause and vibe with the truth, in tech, if you're not learning -

You're not chilling—You are *crashing*.

Skills expire faster than a Netflix trial (2.5 years, per LinkedIn Learning), and titles?

They are just Wi-Fi bars, not the signal.

Your real superpower?

A learning MAP—Mindset, Adaptability, Purpose.

That keeps you coding, building, and flexing in 2025 and beyond neon jungle.

Prashant's story proves it, no degree, micro-courses, community feedback, and two dope projects landed him a Job.

Suppose you are a MIT Person. It is suitable for you. But you do not need MIT.

You need a curious mind, a schedule, and a "never stop" attitude.

This chapter's your cheat code to stay learning, not stuck, with hacks to make it fun, not a grind.

Learning's Your Character, Not Your Title

Tech doesn't stan experience—it stans adaptability.

Quick Stat - *Gartner says 58% of jobs need new skills, and McKinsey's screaming "skill gaps!" at 87% of executives.*

Stack certs like Google Cloud Gen AI or AWS Machine Learning to get noticed but let projects—like a hackathon MVP or open-source PR—make you clutch.

Titles are vibes; learning's the bag that keeps your career 2030-coded.

70/20/10 Is Your OS - Live by the rule

- 70% doing (build a bot, break it, fix it)

- 20% learning from others (mentor DMs, code reviews)

- 10% courses (Coursera, YouTube)

  You cannot YeetCode your way to glory—build, vibe, learn, repeat.

Unlearn to Relearn

The real flex? Dropping ego and old habits. Unlearn "I know enough" or "syntax is king."

Quick Stat- *A 2024 World Economic Forum stat says 44% of skills will shift by 2030.*

Be like Pro, who learned failure's a classroom, not a KO. Reflect weekly, teach a newbie, and keep evolving. Stay stuck in "how it is," and you're AFK in your career.

Do not let your skills 404—learn like your future is on the main net, or you are just a bot stuck in the old meta.

Actions to Lock In the Vibe

#LearnOrLag Challenge: *Pick one skill (e.g., Prompt Engineering). Spend 10 minutes daily on a micro-course (e.g., Vanderbilt's Coursera). Post progress on X with #DigitalHustle.*

Project Sprint: *Build a small project (e.g., a no-code app for a local shop) in 30 days. Push it to GitHub and flex it on LinkedIn: "I just shipped my MVP. Who is next?"*

Mentor Hunt: *DM a tech pro on Discord or LinkedIn: "Yo, how'd you master [skill]?" Share their tips in a study group.*

Sticky Note Swag: *Write "I'll learn fast. I'll apply faster. I'll never stop learning." Slap it on your desk. Say it thrice daily for vibes.*

Key Takeaway: *Learning's the new currency—spend it daily, stack it smart, and you'll code a career that slaps harder than a viral Reels drop.*

Chapter 6

DIGITAL HUSTLE ≠ BURNOUT

"Think of your day like a messy codebase—debug the distractions, commit to what matters, and deploy purposefully. Chaos? That's just unlogged tasks waiting for your spreadsheet sorcery."

– Aalok

Whether you are a Gen Z or Alpha reader or from an older Baby Boomer or Gen-X generation, you are likely deep in the digital grind—coding late, posting on X, or building that side project while balancing a million notifications.

But let's hit pause: does your hustle feel like a fire vibe, or is it burning you out faster than a drained phone battery?

Welcome to *Digital Hustle ≠ Burnout*, where we debunk the myth that grinding 24/7 equals success. It does not. For digital natives like you, the goal is to hustle smart, not hard, and keep your tech journey sustainable, because a burned-out coder cannot change the game.

The hustle culture is authentic, but it is a trap.

Quick Stat: A 2024 Gallup study found that 62% of purpose-driven workers avoid burnout by balancing work and self-care, *something Gen Z and Alpha are wired to prioritize.*

Take Dhruv "D" Carter from Metroplex, who is coming in this chapter. After launching GreenStreak, his recycling app with 50K users, he hit a wall—the servers crashed, and his motivation tanked.

But instead of grinding harder, he took a step back, picked up meditation and sketching, and upskilled in DevOps. That breather did not slow him down—it fueled his comeback.

You are already pros at remixing playlists and adapting to new apps overnight.

This chapter will show you how to remix your hustle—set boundaries, prioritize self-care, and slay your tech goals.

Let's hustle without the burnout, fam, because your glow-up should never come at the cost of your vibe!

Let's go under the Slow Hustle Revolution - The Grind Glitch

In the buzzing heart of Metroplex, 22-year-old **Dhruv**, everyone used to call him "D" Carter, was the poster child for the digital hustle. His X bio screamed *Content Creator | Crypto Bro | 24/7 Grindset*, and his decent followers ate it up.

D churned out vlogs on NFT flips, coded side gigs for startups, and flexed his hustle in aesthetic coffee shop Reels. "Sleep is for the weak," he'd caption, winking at the camera while chugging his third energy drink.

To Gen Z, D was goals—living proof you could Yeet your way to the bag.

But behind the filter, D was a hot mess. His apartment was a warzone of empty Monster cans and unwashed hoodies. He hadn't slept more than four hours in weeks, and his inbox was a nightmare of unread Slack pings.

"This is just the grind," he told himself, ignoring the headaches and that his last real convo with his boys was a blurry Discord call at 2 a.m.

D was sprinting, but to where? He didn't know. All he knew was the mantra: *Keep up or get left.*

One night, mid-stream, D's world glitched. His vision blurred, his hands shook, and his stream crashed as he slumped over his RGB-lit desk. His chat blew up—*Yo, D, you good?*—but he wasn't. His roommate, Jada, a chill graphic designer with a knack for calling out BS, dragged him to urgent care.

The doc's verdict? Burnout, stage critical. "You're running on fumes, kid," she said. "Slow down, or you're gonna crash for real."

D laughed it off, but Jada wasn't having it. "Bro, you're not Tony Stark.

You are one all-nighter away from a full-on L. Have you ever heard of slow hustle?"

D blinked, confused. "Sounds like quitter talk," Jada smirked, tossing him her phone.

On it was a thread from @VibeVault, a lowkey X account dropping wisdom on sustainable grinding.

The tagline hits like a slap: *Hustle hard, but rest harder, or you're just flexing for the void.*

The Boundary Hack, D went home, ego bruised but curious. He scrolled @VibeVault's thread, which broke down the digital hustle trap, the myth that 12-hour days and 2 a.m. emails were the only path to clout.

"Burnout's not a flex," one post read. "76% of y'all are frying your circuits for no reason. Set boundaries, prioritize recovery, and play the long game."

D snorted—boundaries? That was for boomers.

But the stats stuck - *Gen Z's mental health is tanking from hustle culture.*

Slow hustle = sustainable W.

Desperate for a reset, D DM'd @VibeVault. To his shock, they replied, *Meet me at Pixel Café, 3 p.m. Bring a notebook, not your ego.* D showed up, half-expecting a crypto bro in a Lambo hat.

Instead, he met Sage, a 25-year-old ex-influencer turned life coach with box braids and a vibe that screamed , *I had seen the matrix and chose chill.*

"You are Dra, the hustle zombie?" Sage asked, sipping a matcha. D winced. "I'm just… dedicated."

"Dedicated to crashing," Sage shot back. "You are in the digital hustle loop—work, scroll, repeat. No boundaries, no life. Wanna fix it?"

She challenged him to set hard boundaries for one week. *I know you have UK shift hours, no work past 9 p.m., no notifications after hours, and a real workspace, not your bed. Fail, and you'll be just another burnout statistic.*

D took the bait, mostly to prove he was not soft.

Step one: designate work hours. Per Sage's advice, he set 12 p.m. to 9 p.m., blocking out 90-minute sprints with 15-minute breaks. Studies backed this up—focused bursts boosted productivity without frying his brain.

Step two: separate spaces. D turned a corner of his apartment into a legit desk setup, banning his laptop from his couch.

Step three: Muffle the noise. After 7 p.m., he turned off Slack and X notifications, feeling naked but free.

Step four: communicate. He told his clients, "I'm offline in the evenings to recharge. Hit me tomorrow." To his surprise, they respected it.

The first night was strange. D's fingers twitched for his phone, but without notifications, he relaxed. He binged *Arcane*, laughed at memes with Jada, and slept eight hours.

"Eight Hours" - the relief was palpable, a weight lifted from his shoulders.

By day three, he felt sharper, like his brain had rebooted. His vlogs were crisper, his code cleaner.

"Is this what winning feels like?" he posted, half-joking. But deep down, he knew it was. His work was improving, and he was feeling better than ever.

Sage replied: *You're learning, rookie. Keep it up.*

The Slow Hustle Glow-Up, A week in, D was hooked. Sage upped the ante: embraced *slow hustle*—intentional work, deep focus, and recovery as a flex. "Hustle's not about speed," she said. "It's about momentum.

Burnout kills it; recovery fuels it." D nodded, remembering the doc's warning.

Sage gave him a new mission: *Incorporate slow hustle for 30 days.*

Meditate 10 minutes daily, take walks, and pick a hobby. **No multitasking. Deep work only.**

D started small. He downloaded a meditation app, expecting it to be woo-woo nonsense.

But 10 minutes of breathing made his brain feel like it'd been defragged.

He began walking to a nearby park, where there were no AirPods, just vibes. The world felt louder—birds, traffic, his thoughts.

He picked up sketching as a hobby, doodling cyberpunk cityscapes. It was not for clout; it was for him. Jada caught him sketching and grinned.

"Yo, you're giving main character energy now, not NPC."

Deep work was the real game-changer. D blocked two-hour chunks for coding, turning off Wi-Fi to dodge distractions. He read about Cal Newport's *Deep Work* and became obsessed.

No more tab-switching or "quick X checks." His output soared— apps debugged faster, vlogs edited in half the time.

Sage shared a Gallup stat that stuck with him: *42% of tech workers feel mentally drained daily.* D wasn't about to be that guy.

One night, D hit a wall. A client demanded a same-day turnaround, and old habits screamed, *Grind now, sleep never.*

But Sage's voice echoed: *Rest is strategy.* D negotiated a deadline for the next day, took a 15-minute nap, and crushed the project fresh.

The client was stoked, and D realized that boundaries didn't make him weak—they made him clutch.

The Hackathon Heist, A month later, Sage dropped a bombshell: Metroplex was hosting *Hack the Future*, a 72-hour hackathon for young creators.

The prize? Seed funding for a startup and a feature on X's trending page.

D's eyes lit up—this was his shot to level up.

But the competition was stacked: Ivy League coders, YouTube-famous devs, and corporate-backed squads with infinite Red Bull.

Sage smirked. "You're ready, D. Slow hustle's your cheat code."

D teamed up with Jada and two Nexus recruits: Leo, a UI designer with a knack for clean aesthetics, and Amara, a data scientist who could make algorithms sing.

They called themselves *ChillCoders*, a nod to their vibe.

Their idea? *VibeSync* is an app that gamifies work—life balance by tracking work hours, nudging users to rest, and rewarding recovery with streaks and badges.

"It is like Duolingo for not burning out," Jada pitched, and the team was sold.

The hackathon was chaos. Teams chugged espresso and coded like their lives depended on it. ChillCoders, though, stuck to their slow hustle playbook.

They worked in 90-minute sprints, took walks between sessions, and banned all-nighters.

D led the backend, coding VibeSync's core logic. Jada designed a clean UI that could've starred in a Wes Anderson flick. Leo polished the front end, and Amara's algorithms predicted burnout risks with scary accuracy.

At hour 50, disaster struck. Their server crashed, wiping out half their progress. The team panic, but D channeled Sage, *Focusing on recovery and rebuilding*.

They took a 20-minute breather, sketched a recovery plan, and dove back in.

D's deep work muscle kicked in, and he rewrote the backend in record time. Jada's mockups were flawless, and Amara's data models hummed.

By demo day, VibeSync was live—a slick, gamified app that screamed *Gen Z but made it healthy.*

The judges, a mix of tech CEOs and X influencers, were shocked.

"You built this in 72 hours *and* stayed chill?" one asked. D grinned. "Slow hustle, fam.

Work smart, rest hard." ChillCoders took first place, snagging $50K in funding and a viral X thread that blew up D's notifications.

This time, he muted them and celebrated IRL with pizza and his squad.

The Long Game, A year later, D was a new man. VibeSync was Metroplex's hottest startup, with 100K downloads and a TED Talk invite.

D still vlogged, but his content had evolved—tutorials on slow hustle, mental health hacks, and why rest was the ultimate flex.

His followers doubled, not from flexing the grind set but from keeping it real.

"Burnout's not a badge," he posted. Balance is the bag."

D's apartment was now a vibe: plants, a legit desk, and a no-phones-after-8 rule. He and Jada were planning VibeSync 2.0, with Leo and Amara as co-founders.

Sage became their mentor, dropping gems like, "Success isn't a sprint; it's a wave.

Ride it, do not drown." D's mental health was solid, and his hustle was sustainable. He even started mentoring kids at Nexus, teaching them to code and chill.

One night, at Pixel Café, D toasted with Sage. "Thought I'd be stuck in the grind glitch forever," he said. Sage laughed.

"You hacked the real game, D—your life. What's next?" D smirked. "World domination, but, like, at a chill pace."

The epilogue, the Moral, is (Dhruv) "D's" story, a Gen Z wake-up call.

The digital hustle can be a trap if you let it run amok

Slow hustle is not just a hack—it is a lifestyle. So, choose your vibe: burn *out chasing clout, or glow up playing the long game.*

Success is not about grinding till you break; it is about boundaries, deep work, and rest as a power move.

Remember—*you cannot flex a W if you run on E, fam. Hustle slow, rest bold, or get ghosted by your glow-up.*

Digital Hustle ≠ Burnout

Setting Boundaries and Practicing Slow Hustle for Long-Term Momentum.

The Truth About the Digital Hustle

In today's world, the concept of the "hustle" has been romanticized. It's become a badge of honor to work 12-hour days, answer emails at 2 a.m., and turn every waking moment into an opportunity to "grind."

We see the success stories of those who pushed themselves to the limit and think, "That's the only way to make it."

But here's the thing, **Digital Hustle ≠ Burnout.**

A stark difference exists between working hard and overexerting oneself.

The hustle is not the problem; the lack of balance leads to burnout. And the worst part?

Burnout does not just slow you down—it crushes your momentum, and it's a serious issue we need to address.

Quick Stat - *According to Gallup, a staggering 76% of workers experience burnout at some point in their careers, and it's even more prevalent in our younger generations, who are facing a mental health crisis tied directly to the pressure of constant work and perfectionism.*

Gen Z, in particular, is facing a mental health crisis tied directly to the pressure of constant work and perfectionism.

The key to long-term success is not running yourself ragged. It's setting boundaries and practicing slow hustle—a sustainable, intentional pace built for recovery.

Setting Boundaries in Remote and Hybrid Hustle Culture

Remote and hybrid work have revolutionized the way we work.

The ability to work from anywhere sounds like freedom, but it can also create a never-ending loop of work. When your workspace is also your living space, the lines blur.

The same device you use to check your emails can quickly become a distraction, pulling you back into "work mode" at all hours.

This is where strong boundaries step in—

It is not about being inflexible.

It is about owning time, protecting energy, and prioritizing well-being.

It is the freedom to say "no" without guilt—and the power to mean it.

Here's how to set boundaries to thrive, not just survive

- **Designate Work Hours:** Just because you can work 24/7 does not mean you should. Set a clear start and end time for your workday and communicate it to your team. If your schedule allows, try working in blocks of 90 minutes, followed by breaks.

Research backs this up—this approach does not just boost productivity; it also acts like burnout's kryptonite while preventing it.

- **Separate Workspace and Living Space:** If you work from home, create a physical boundary between your work and living areas to maintain a clear distinction between the two. This will signal to your brain when it's time to "switch off" and give you a sense of closure at the end of the day.

- **Turn Off Notifications:** Stop letting the digital world dictate your every move. Mute non-essential notifications. It is okay not to respond immediately—people respect your boundaries when you show them you appreciate them.

- **Communicate Expectations Clearly:** Set clear expectations for yourself and others to ensure mutual understanding and alignment. Let your colleagues know when you're unavailable and be firm but fair about the time you give to work.

Let's take Sophia, a young digital marketer, for example. She constantly checked emails at 11 p.m., thinking it was "normal." She realized that it was stealing her downtime and affecting her sleep.

By setting a boundary to turn off her notifications after 7 p.m. and communicating this to her team, she became more energized during work hours and increased her productivity. Her performance did not dip—it improved.

The Power of Slow Hustle: Recovery for Long-Term Momentum

The "slow hustle" is the antidote to the burnout culture. It is about doing less but doing it with more purpose and intention.

Slow hustle is about playing the long game and recognizing that momentum is built in waves, not sprinting to a finish line.

Here's why the slow hustle works and how you can incorporate it into your routine

- **Focus on Recovery, Not Just Work:** The idea of "hustling" does not have to mean grinding nonstop. Recovery is one of the most critical parts of the hustle.

- Constant work without recovery leads to diminishing returns.

- Slow hustle practices like meditation, walking, and hobbies outside of work can refuel your mental and physical energy.

Quick Stat - *In the tech industry, 42% of workers report feeling mentally drained at the end of a typical workday, and 27% say they feel emotionally exhausted.*

Think of recovery as an investment in your future productivity

- **Prioritize Deep Work:** Slow hustle emphasizes focus over quantity. The idea of working smarter rather than harder is crucial.

- In the age of constant distractions, adopting a deep work mindset—where you dedicate undisturbed time to critical tasks—can make you much more efficient. Importantly, it prevents burnout from multitasking.

- To learn more about deep work, I recommend reading *Cal Newport's book "Deep Work."*

- **Embrace Rest as a Strategy:** Rest is not the enemy of productivity. It is the essential ingredient for sustained creativity and output.

- Tim Ferriss, author of *"The 4-Hour Workweek"*, advocates for taking long breaks, practicing "doing nothing," and allowing yourself to recharge fully.

- Research from the University of Illinois has shown that taking breaks and allowing your mind to wander can increase creative thinking and problem-solving.

Let's read an example: Jake, a software engineer, worked 12-hour days to meet deadlines. He found himself exhausted and less motivated.

After reading about the benefits of deep work and slow hustle, he took 15-minute breaks every two hours to rest his brain.

He started sleeping better, his focus improved, and his work output skyrocketed.

Inspiring Long-Term Change: Making Slow Hustle a Lifestyle

If there is one thing you should take away from this, slow hustle is not a temporary fix but *a lifestyle change.*

You must make it part of your routine and redefine what success looks like to you.

It is not about burning out to prove you are working hard. It is about creating a career where you can sustainably innovate, grow, and enjoy the process.

Quick Stat - *A report by Deloitte shows that 84% of Gen Z workers want a job that promotes work-life balance, which is directly tied to avoiding burnout.*

The good news is that more and more companies are recognizing this shift.

You can contribute to this change by committing to purposeful hustle, which involves setting boundaries, prioritizing recovery, and focusing on sustainable growth over instant gratification.

Ready to draw the line?

Here are some down-to-earth, doable boundary-setting habits you can weave into your daily grind to protect your peace, keep burnout at bay, and live after work.

The Time-Blocking Exercise (This is My Favorite)

What it is: Time blocking involves scheduling specific blocks for different tasks throughout your day. It is a straightforward way to set boundaries around when you will be working, resting, or doing other activities.

How to do it

Start with your work tasks: Identify the tasks you must complete during your day and block out specific times to work on them.

Set boundaries for personal time: Block out time for breaks, meals, and individual activities.

Stick to the plan: Visualize your day using a digital calendar or a planner. Stick to the boundaries you've set—when the work block is over, switch off and transition to the next task.

Why it works: This exercise helps you intentionally prioritize your time, ensuring that work does not spill over into your personal life. Carving out time to recharge also reduces the risk of burnout.

The No-Work Zone Exercise

What it is: Designating a specific physical or mental space where no work is allowed can be a great way to set boundaries, especially if you're working from home.

How to do it

Choose a space: Choose a place in your home free of work-related distractions, such as your bedroom, living room, or a specific area.

Make it a "no-work" zone: This space is for Rest, relaxation, or activities that nourish your well-being. Leave your laptop and phone outside this space.

Communicate your boundaries: Let those around you (family, friends, or housemates) know that when you are in this space, it is personal time.

Why it works: This exercise creates a physical boundary between work and Rest, helping your mind understand that some spaces are reserved solely for recovery.

The Technology Shutdown Exercise (Practices Daily or at least on weekends)

What it is: Set time each day to shut off all work-related technology completely—this could include your work phone, laptop, and any apps related to work communication.

How to do it

Call it a wrap, on your terms: Pick a time that works for you—say, 7 p.m. sharp—and treat it like a digital curfew. That means no more emails, no Slack pings, no "just one last thing" syndrome.

Set your shutdown ritual: Let your phone or calendar app be your accountability buddy. Schedule a gentle nudge to power down, step away, and reclaim your evening.

Swap screens for soul food: Trade that doom-scroll time for something that fuels you, whether it is a workout, a book that isn't on Kindle, or diving into that dusty old hobby you keep saying you'll get back to.

Why it works: This exercise helps you disconnect from the digital world, which can often blur the lines between personal and professional time. It helps reduce stress and foster a healthy work-life balance.

The "No Meetings" Day Exercise (Try this if this is in your control area)

What it is: A day free of meetings can help you regain control of your time and reduce the feeling of constant digital hustle.

How to do it

Pick your no-meeting day: Claim one day a week—say, Friday—as your sacred no-meeting zone. Block it off like your productivity depends on it (because it does).

Make it count: Use that quiet space to dive deep into work that matters—those tasks you keep pushing, the creative stuff, or heck, even a well-earned breather.

Loop in the crew: Let your team know you are going dark on meetings that day. This will set the tone and inspire them to guard their focus time.

Why it works: This exercise helps you carve out uninterrupted work time to focus on your most important tasks. It can also help reduce the mental strain of constant back-to-back meetings.

The "Prioritize and Say No" Exercise (Learn to Say No Without Losing Reputation)

What it is: Learning to say no is essential to setting boundaries, especially in a remote or hybrid work environment where expectations can sometimes feel overwhelming.

How to do it

Lock in your weekly game plan: Every Monday (or whatever day feels like your reset), jot down your top priorities. What is mission-critical? What moves the needle toward your bigger goals? That is your north star.

Filter the noise: When new requests land on your plate, gut-check them. Do they line up with your priorities? If not, do not hesitate to say "not now" or renegotiate the timeline. Protect your focus like it is premium real estate—because it is.

Be upfront, stay firm: Set the tone early. Let your team know what's realistic for you and when. Clarity beats burnout, and firm boundaries build trust.

Why it hits different: Learning to say "no" isn't rude—it's a power move. It guards your time, saves energy, and reminds you (and others) that your focus is reserved for the work that moves the needle.

The Reflect and Recharge Exercise (This is most Critical, It Is Soul)

- **What it is:** Regular self-reflection can help you evaluate how well you stick to your boundaries and recharge when necessary.

How to do it

Set time for reflection: At the end of each week, take 10-15 minutes to assess how you have handled your boundaries. Did you stick to your time blocks? Did you allow work to creep into personal space? Setting clear work-life boundaries is crucial to maintaining a healthy balance.

Recharge code: What fuels your spirit outside the grind? Maybe it is a long walk, a sweaty workout, kitchen chaos with family, or getting lost in a creative flow. Whatever it is, do not leave it to chance—build it into your weekends and downtime like it matters (because it does).

Breaks are not some optional luxury—they are the reboot button your brain desperately needs.

Stepping back is not falling behind.

It is how you come back stronger, calmer, and ready to own your lane.

Evaluate progress: Tracking your ability to set and maintain boundaries over time and adjusting as needed gives you control over your time and energy. This empowerment significantly improves your work-life balance.

Why it works?

This exercise helps you stay mindful about your boundaries and gives you the space to recharge when needed. It keeps you accountable for yourself and your goals.

Reflecting on your work also gives you a sense of achievement as you see how far you've come and your progress in maintaining your boundaries.

By consistently practicing these exercises, you'll set more precise boundaries and build a more sustainable, fulfilling routine that protects your well-being while enabling long-term success.

Organize Your Day Like a Tech Boss

Yo, Gen Z and Alpha, if your workday feels like a Discord server with 50 unread channels,

Let us debug that chaos.

I have learned the hard way as a Senior Oracle DBA, a messy day thanks to your vibe and output.

So, here is my battle-tested hack to organize your day like a tech boss, whether you are a junior dev or a cloud newbie.

Let's understand this, your shift starts at 12 p.m.

Get in 30 minutes early—yep, sacrifice that extra Insta scroll—and time-block 20 minutes to craft a to-do list that slaps.

This is not just a list. It is your daily MVP, keeping you clutch in the IT grind.

Let us break it down with simple steps, tools, and my Excel-fueled routine to keep your day 2030-coded.

Tools You will need: Grab a notebook and pen for old-school vibes, or go digital with Excel, Word, Outlook's To-Do feature, or Notepad.

Me? I'm an Excel stan—spreadsheets are my love language. Pick what vibes with you but keep it consistent.

My Three-Step Playbook (with a side of Aalok's chaos):

Step one: Eat the Ugly Frog First

Start by tackling the task that stresses you most—what productivity guru Brian Tracy calls your "ugly frog."

It is usually a pending database migration that's been haunting my inbox.

In your case, it could be that one bug in your code that you've been avoiding or that difficult email you need to send.

Open Excel and create a sheet with columns –

Task, Date, Priority (High/Medium/Low), Status.

Drop that frog at the top, like "Fix schema bug—May 16—High—In Progress." Pro tip: Naming the beast kills stress.

Quick Stat – *A 2024 Harvard study says tackling high-priority tasks early boosts focus by 60%. Eat that frog, fam, and the rest of your day will be a breeze.*

Step two: Tame the Email Jungle

Emails are a trap—some are FYIs, some are action items, and some are just HR flexing new policies. Sort them by priority: high (client, boss), Medium (colleagues), Low (newsletters).

For each, ask: Is this info to consume, an action to execute, or a follow-up to chase? Copy the subject line into your Excel sheet, adding Owner (you or someone else), Action Type (e.g., "Reply," "Code"), and Due Date.

No due date? Add a remark like "Need response by?"

and ping the sender. Set up Outlook folders: Client, Boss/Lead, Team, HR, and Inbox for randoms.

Use rules to auto-sort emails from VIPs.

Quick Stat: A 2023 McKinsey study says organized email workflows save 10 hours a week. Stop drowning and *start slaying.*

Step three: Check in Frequently

Visit your Excel sheet three times a day, at the start of the shift (plan), midday (pivot), and at the end of the day (review).

Mark tasks such as Done, Pushed, or WIP.

Midday, reassess priorities—maybe that "Low" bug is now a client fire.

At day's end, log what's done and what's sliding to tomorrow. This is not just admin.

It is your victory lap.

Quick Stat- *A 2024 LinkedIn study says daily task reviews boost productivity by 45%. Close your day knowing you shipped, not just showed up.*

My Excel Format (Steal This)

Task	Date	Priority	Owner	Action Type	Due Date	Status	Remarks
Fix schema bug	**May 16**	High-P1	Name	Code	May 17	**In Progress**	Client escalation
Reply to the boss's SLA query.	May 16	High – P2	Name	Reply	May 16	Done	Sent at 2 p.m.
Team sync notes	May 16	Medium – P3	Name	Consume	-	Done	Info only
Send Meeting Invite for Code review with Client	Jun 4	High – P2	Name	Review	Jun 10	Open	code fix release in Q2

Why Slaps?

This system is not about micromanaging—it is about owning your day like a tech lead owns a sprint.

It is flexible for coders, analysts, or cloud newbies and scales with your hustle. Gen Z and Alpha, you are built for this—multitasking like you are modding Minecraft while streaming on Twitch.

Remember—don't let your day 500—time block *like a boss, eat frogs for breakfast, and code a workday that slaps harder than a viral Git commit.*

CONCLUSION

Let's close this chapter with a real one—time for a vibe test.

Yeah, the digital hustle is wild and full of opportunity, but burnout?

That is a hard no.

You are out here to build, code, and design your future in the fast Glow of 2025 and beyond neon grind. But here's the truth: The real flex is the slow hustle—moving with purpose, setting your own pace, and building something that won't just spark but *sustain.*

Forget the clout-chasing, 2 a.m. email life.

That is a one-way ticket to a crash.

Quick Stat - *Gallup's 2024 stat says 76% of workers hit burnout, and Gen Z is feeling the heat hardest, with mental health struggles tied to always-on perfectionism.*

But you are not here to sprint 'til you snap—you are here to glow up for the long game.

This conclusion is your MAP (Mindset, Adaptability, Purpose) to hustle smart, rest bold, and code a career that slaps without stealing your Soul.

LET'S BREAK IT DOWN WITH FOUR CLUTCH POINTS FOR DAILY PRACTICES

Boundaries Are Your Superpower

- Remote work has a vibe but is also a trap—your laptop is not your BFF at 11 p.m. Sophia, our digital marketer, learned this when she muted notifications after 7 p.m., boosting her energy and output.

- Set boundaries like a tech boss: time-block work hours (90-minute sprints, per studies, slay productivity), carve out a no-work zone (bedroom for Netflix, not Jira), and mute Slack pings after hours.

- Communicate your limits—clients respect a "brb, I'm human" vibe.

Remember - *Boundaries are not walls—they are the Wi-Fi password to your mental bandwidth.*

Quick Stat- *A 2023 Deloitte stat says 84% of you want jobs with work-life balance, and companies are catching up—60% of Gen Z pick employers who vibe with flexibility.*

Slow Hustle = Long-Term W

- Slow hustle is not lazy—it is strategic. Jake, our coder, swapped 12-hour death marches for 15-minute breaks every two hours, and his focus went God-mode.

- Prioritize deep work (shoutout Cal Newport) over multitasking chaos. Focus on one task, like debugging a feature, for 90 minutes—your brain is not a TikTok algorithm.

- Recovery is your secret Sauce. Meditation, walks, or gaming sessions recharge your grind.

- Tim Ferriss says "do nothing" sometimes; it is not slacking but investing in your next commitment.

Remember - *Slow hustles like a well-timed respawn—rest, reload, and frag the game.*

Quick Stat - *A 2024 University of Illinois study says breaks spark creativity and problem-solving, while 42% of tech workers feel drained without them.*

Own Your Day Like a Tech Lead

- Your day is a codebase—debug it or crash. My Excel-fueled routine (from "Organize Your Day Like a Tech Boss") keeps chaos in check: eat your "ugly frog" (the most enormous task) first, tame emails with priority folders, and check your to-do list thrice daily.

- Sophia's no-notifications rule and Jake's break schedule show how owning your day saves energy for deep work and life. Gen Z, you're multitasking pros—use that Minecraft-modding energy to slay your schedule.

Remember - *A messy day's a 500 error—time-block like a pro and ship commits, not stress.*

Quick Stat - *A 2024 LinkedIn stat says structured days boost productivity by 45%. Start your shift early, time-block 20 minutes for a to-do list, and sort tasks by High/Medium/Low.*

Make Slow Hustle Your Lifestyle

- Slow hustle is not a hack—it's your OS. Redefine success as sustainable growth, not burnout badges.

- You're building a career, not a sprint. Say no to tasks that don't vibe with your goals (politely, no rep loss).

- Embrace rest as a strategy, not a weakness. Your hustle's a playlist—curate it with intention, and it'll slap for decades.

Remember – *Burnout is for bots—code a hustle that glows without going ghost.*

Quick Stat - *A 2024 Pew study says 70% of you crave structure and balance—lean into it. Reflect weekly: Did I set boundaries? Did I recharge? Adjust like you're patching a bug. Sophia and Jake didn't just survive—they thrived by prioritizing energy over output.*

Key Takeaways

- **Protect Your Energy**: *Your vibe is your most clutch resource. To guard it, set one boundary daily (e.g., no work after 8 p.m.).*

- **Rest Is Power**: *Schedule 15-minute breaks every two hours—walk, stretch, or vibe to lo-fi. It's your brain's debug mode.*
- **Own Your Rhythm**: *Time-block one high-priority task (your "ugly frog") each morning. Could you ship it, flex it, repeat?*
- **Reflect & Recharge**: *End your week with a 10-minute vibe check: What worked? What drained me? Plan one recovery activity (e.g., gaming, hiking).*

Remember—digital hustle is Your Art, Not Your Cage. Paint it with boundaries, rest, and intention to build a career that's fire without burnout. Your energy is the genuine bag. Spend *it slow, stack it smart, and glow up for the long haul.*

And do not let burnout DDoS ruin your dreams—

Hustles slow with *"Purpose and Make It Mean Something,"* rest clutch, and code a legacy that crashes Basic's servers, leaving the algorithm shaken.

Actions to Lock in the Slow Hustle Vibe

#SlowHustleChallenge: *Time-block your day tomorrow with 90-minute work sprints and 15-minute breaks. Post your schedule on X with #DigitalHustle: "Hustling slow, glowing hard."*

No-Work Zone Flex: *Pick a spot (e.g., the couch) as your no-work zone. Spend 30 minutes there tonight, tech-free—read, vibe, or nap. Share the vibe online: "My couch is my sanctuary? What's yours?"*

Say-No Script: *Write a polite "no" for a low-priority task (e.g., "Thanks, but I'm swamped—can we revisit next week?"). Use it this week and DM a work bestie: "Just said no, still got clout!"*

Recharge Ritual: *Pick one recovery activity (e.g., 10-minute Meditation, skate session). Do it daily for a week. Flex it on LinkedIn: "Meditation's my new commitment—what's your recharge? #SlowHustle."*

Vibe-Check Journal: *Every Sunday, jot down one boundary you set and one way you recharged. Tweak next week's plan to keep the hustle sustainable.*

#DayBoss Challenge: *Start tomorrow's shift 30 minutes early. Time-block 20 minutes to build your to-do list in Excel or Notepad. Post your setup on X with #DigitalHustle: "Just ate my next frog? ☒"*

Email Glow-Up: *Create three Outlook folders (Client, Boss, Team) and one rule (e.g., auto-sort boss's emails). Log one action item in your to-do list today.*

Frog Hunt: *Write down one "ugly frog" task you've dodged. Add it to your list with a due date. Tackle it first tomorrow and DM a work bestie: "Frog down, vibes up!"*

Read Books: *I highly recommend Brian Tracy's book EAT THAT FROG. It's an excellent read for anyone looking to boost their productivity and conquer their most challenging tasks.*

PART III

PURPOSE—MAKE IT MEAN SOMETHING

"From Passion to Purpose, it is not just a vibe—it is the code that transforms your hustle into a legacy. Code for a cause, not clout, and watch your IT Game Reshape The World."

– Aalok

IS THE PURPOSE TO MAKE IT MEAN SOMETHING? LET'S CHECK THE VIBE OF YOUR LIFE

Yo, Gen Z, let us have a real one.

You are out here slaying—coding apps in your dorm, dropping fire Reels that hit a milli, or grinding side hustles to flex on the 'Gram.

You are the generation that turned "vibe" into a personality and "hustle" into a religion.

But let us pause the scroll and vibe-check your soul for a sec.

What is it all *for?*

Are you building something that slaps or just chasing clout in a digital hamster wheel?

If your grind does not have a *why?* You are one algorithm tweak away from a full-on existential L.

WELCOME TO THE GAME CHANGER - PURPOSE

Not the corny, boomer "find your calling" nonsense, but the kind of purpose that is like a double-shot espresso for your soul.

It is the fire that makes your code, your art, your hustle *mean* something—something bigger than likes, followers, or a fat Venmo deposit.

The Purpose is the ultimate Gen Z hack; it keeps you lit when the Wi-Fi is down, the haters are loud, and your energy is running on a 2% battery.

And in the wild, neon-lit jungle of tech, where every day's a new flex or flop.

The purpose is your North Star, your Discord mod, and your *reason to keep it 100*.

Picture this: it is 2025, Metroplex, the city that never logs off.

Dhurv "D" Carter, our slow-hustle king from *VibeSync*, is chilling at Pixel Café, his go-to spot for matcha and real talk. D is a Gen Z legend now with 80K followers, a startup trending on X, and a clean vibe he could sell as an NFT.

But tonight, he's shook. His RGB keyboard is collecting dust, his inbox is a warzone, and his latest vlog barely cracked 100K views.

"I'm out here grinding," he mutters, staring into his latte art like it's a crystal ball.

"But *what is the point?* Am I just a content machine for the void?"

Enter Sage, the ex-influencer turned life-coach GOAT, with braids bluer than a verified checkmark and wisdom sharper than a 4K monitor. She slides into the booth, clocks D's vibe, and goes, "Bruh, you are in a clout coma.

Your passions are in life support, and you are one all-nighter from a hard crash.

You need *purpose*—the kind that makes your hustle hit different." D squints, skeptical.

Purpose? That's giving TED Talk vibes.

I'm just tryna code and get paid."

Sage smirked, leaning in like she was about to drop a secret cheat code.

"Passion is the spark," D. It gets you hyped.

But "Purpose? That is the fire."

You keep grinding when the likes dry up and the bugs pile up.

Without it, you are just flexing for the algorithm.

Sage's words hit D like a 360 no-scope. He had been riding the passion wave—coding *VibeSync*, gamifying work-life balance, and preaching slow hustle to his squad. Lately, though, it has felt like a loop: code, post, repeat.

His spark was fizzling, and the grind was starting to feel like a YouTube trend he was late to. Sage was not done.

She pulled out her phone, showing him a stat from a 2023 Deloitte survey: *84% of Gen Z want jobs with social impact, and 67% pick purpose over pay.*

"Your generation is built differently," she said.

You do not just want a bag. You want a Legacy.

But you gotta find your *why* first."

D was not sold yet. "Okay, but how? Tech is a circus—AI, crypto, cybersecurity, AR. Everyone's shouting, 'This is the move!' I'm just tryna not flop."

Sage grinned, tossing him a napkin with a scribbled challenge, *One month. Find a purpose that makes your hustle mean something. Align your skills with a real-world need—climate, equity, health, whatever slaps— code for a cause, not just clout.*

D stared at the napkin, heart racing. This was not a coding sprint or a hackathon, but a vibe check for his entire life.

Let us break it down for you, Gen Z.

The purpose is not some dusty self-help book your mom keeps on the shelf.

It answers the 3 a.m. question: *Why am I doing this?*

In tech, where you can build anything from a meme coin to a life-saving app, purpose separates the NPCs (Non-Playable Characters) from the main characters.

Passion got you into- you may love gaming, so you started modding Minecraft, or you were obsessed with anime and dove into AR filters.

That is the spark. But purpose? That is when you point those skills at something that matters, like coding an app that tracks carbon footprints or securing data for a nonprofit. It is the difference between a viral moment and a movement.

If I talk real talk, the world is a mess, and Gen Z knows it. Climate is glitching, mental health is in the red, and half the internet is a scam.

Quick Stat: *A 2022 Pew Research study says 70% of you want tech to fix climate change, and 65% are hyped about using AI for social good.*

That is your superpower—you see the chaos and wanna code the fix. But here is the tea (truth), purpose does not just *happen*. You gotta hunt for it, like a rare skin in a battle royale.

Here is the crux, purpose is crafted, not found by chance.

And in tech, the hunt means aligning your hype (gaming, art, memes) with real-world needs (healthcare, education, sustainability).

Take Lina K, a Gen Z coder who turned her API obsession into a purpose. She started building slick e-commerce apps, but it felt like selling her soul for clicks. Then she found *tech-for-good*—using code to solve IRL problems.

Lina pivoted to open-source disaster relief apps, mapping safe routes during floods.

Her passion for APIs was the spark, her purpose—saving lives—was the fire.

Now, her code powers NGOs in Southeast Asia, and she is an example of how you can flex your skills *and* make a dent in the universe.

D felt that energy. He loved gaming and community vibes, so Sage pushed him to explore tech for good. He stumbled upon gamification, which uses game mechanics to make boring or mundane task more engaging and fun.

What if he coded an app that turned recycling into a Fortnite-style quest, with skins for sorting plastic?

The idea lit him up, not because it'd go viral, but because it could change how his city rolled. That is the purpose **when your hustle feels like a mission, not a flex.**

So, Gen Z, here is the deal: your purpose is out there, waiting in the overlap of what you love and the world needs. It is not about ditching your vibe but leveling it up. You do not have to save the planet (unless that's your thing).

Your purpose may be teaching kids to code, securing data from hackers, or building AR worlds for storytellers. Whatever it is, it has to make your heart race and your code compile.

Because in 2025, the real flex is not a blue checkmark—it's why that makes your hustle immortal.

Remember—*passion is the YouTube trend that gets you moving, and Purpose is the anthem that keeps you grooving. Find your why, or are you just dancing for the void?*

QUICK HACK FOR GEN Z

Grab your Notes app.

Write three things you are obsessed with (games, music, memes) and three world problems you'd Yeet out of existence (pollution, inequality, bad Wi-Fi).

WHERE DO THEY OVERLAP?

That is your purpose starter pack. Google one idea, join a Discord, and vibe-check it in real life.

If you still need help, jump into the chapter to see the simplified **"Purpose Map."**

Chapter 7

PASSION IS A SPARK, PURPOSE IS THE FIRE

"Passion Sparks Purpose, Purpose blooms Meaning—and in Meaning, I find my Solace."

– Aalok

We all begin somewhere—with a spark. It might hit you the first time you cracked a problem in code at 2 a.m., built something extraordinary in a weekend hackathon.

Or customized a game mod that made your friends say, "Whoa, you did that?"

That *spark*—that feeling of *"this is so me"*—is passion.

It is the high-energy jolt that gets you started in tech. And it is powerful.

But let us be real, passion alone is not enough to go the distance.

Because passion is loud, messy, exciting, and sometimes short-lived, it is like a burst of Wi-Fi in a remote area, thrilling while it lasts, but not something you can rely on to carry you through the grind.

One rugged sprint, one boring project, or one manager who does not "get it," and boom—your spark dims.

That is where so many talented people start to question themselves. "Maybe I'm not cut out for this." But the problem is not you.

It is that no one taught you how to turn passion into purpose.

See, **passion *starts* the journey. Purpose *sustains* it**.

The purpose is deeper.

It is the engine that keeps running long after the caffeine crash and the initial hype fades.

It is that quiet conviction when you wake up thinking, *"This thing I'm building—it matters to me."* Not every gig will be glamorous. Not every task will light you up.

But you move intentionally when locked into your *why?* Even through the messy, unfiltered parts. And no, that's not just feel-good talk.

That is the real difference between burning out and leveling up. It is how the ones who *last* in this game play it smartly.

And no, purpose does not have to be some grand, save-the-world thing. It can be as real and grounded as:

- *"I want to use tech to help small businesses grow."*
- *"I want to build tools that solve real problems in my community."*
- *"I want financial freedom doing what I love."*
- *"I want to prove to myself I can do this—on my terms."*

Purpose transforms hustle into direction. It is the shift from *doing more* to *doing what truly matters*.

Where passion strikes the first spark, the purpose is the steady flame—it powers you through late nights, looming deadlines, imposter syndrome, and every "Am I even good enough?" moment.

The compass cuts through the chaos and keeps you grounded in an industry that never stops moving.

In this chapter, we will unpack how to uncover your purpose without stressing about having all the answers upfront.

We will explore how to sync your everyday grind with your bigger vision, manage burnout before it takes over, and carve out a tech career that's not just loud with hype, but rich with meaning.

The discussion is practical, actionable, and designed to give you the confidence to navigate your career with purpose.

Because here is the truth: When your passion connects with purpose, you stop drifting and start *driving* your path forward.

Because in 2025's tech world, anyone can be busy.

But those who stay lit for the long haul?

They are not chasing passion.

They are anchored on purpose.

Let us figure out what that looks like for *you*. Before we discuss how to align purpose and personal interests with real-world IT needs, let us understand -

What Does "Purpose" Even Mean Anymore? Is it a search to find a meaning in life?

These questions have a strong Spiritual aspect. However, this book will cover only what is relevant to IT Job seekers.

Define Purpose: How to Start? To define the purpose, ask yourself -

- What makes me come alive? (What energizes me?)
- What do I deeply care about? (Causes, problems, communities)
- What are my strengths or growing skills? (What do others value in me?)

- What impact do I want to make? (How do I want the world to change because I was here?)

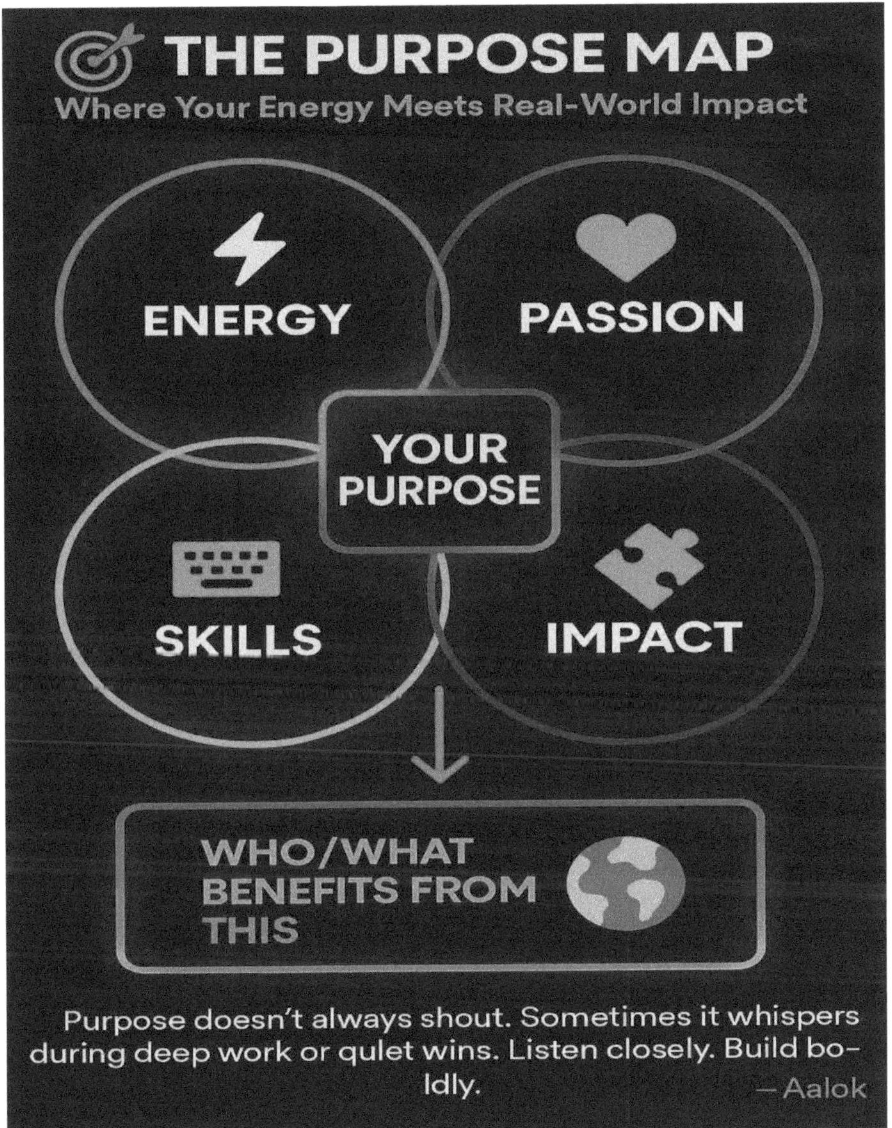

STEP-BY-STEP: HOW TO USE THE PURPOSE MAP

Identify Your ENERGY

Ask

- What activities energize me, even after hours of doing them?
- When do I feel most alive, alert, or in flow?

Look for moments when time flies. That is your energy zone.

Clarify Your PASSION

Ask

- What topics or causes do I deeply care about?
- What do I naturally talk or read about, even if no one pays me?

This is not a one-time answer. Passions evolve. Follow your curiosity breadcrumbs.

Audit Your SKILLS

Ask

- What am I good at? What do others often come to me for help with?
- What skills have I developed that feel natural or come more easily to me than others?

Do not just focus on hard skills (coding, design). Include soft skills (communication, leadership) as well.

Pinpoint Your IMPACT

Ask

- Where does my work make a difference?
- What problems do I feel called to solve?

The Purpose is tied to contribution. Think of who or what benefits from your effort.

Find the OVERLAP: Your Purpose

Look at where Energy, Passion, Skills, and Impact intersect.

That's your sweet spot—your purpose.

You do not need all four to be perfect. Start where there is a substantial overlap and evolve.

Test It: Who/What Benefits from This?

Ask

- If I doubled down on this, who would help?
- Can this create value in someone else's life, team, or community?

  Purpose is not just about you; it is about usefulness. Make it matter.

Start Small, Reflect Often

- Purpose doesn't always arrive loud & clear. Sometimes it whispers.
- Pay attention to patterns in your work, fulfillment, and feedback from others.

  Build quietly. Build boldly. Adjust as you grow.

Let us reiterate that when all three overlap, you have found PURPOSE

That center zone is fixed.

It evolves as you grow. However, the more time you spend in that space, the more energized, useful, and fulfilled you will feel.

Remember—purpose does not always shout. Sometimes, *it whispers during deep work, quiet wins, or when someone says, 'That helped me.' Listen closely. Build boldly. This emphasis on mindfulness and attentiveness will help you uncover your purpose in unexpected places.*

Align the Purpose and Personal Interest Worksheet

The goal here is to discover the overlap between what you love, what you are good at, what the world needs, and where you can make an impact.

As an example, I filled in an example view to understand better-

---

PART 1: PERSONAL INTERESTS

List 5-10 things you are genuinely curious about or enjoy doing.

What energizes you, even when no one's watching?

List your tasks

1. Love talking to people
2. Documenting
3. Script to Automate tough

PART 2: ENERGY ZONES

From the list above, mark the ones that energize you the most.

When do you feel most in flow or "on fire"?

Describe 2-3 recent moments.

Example

1. I feel in the flow when teaching others how to use new tech tools or designing an intuitive UI.
2. I feel better when I automate my manual DB refresh process.
3. I feel confident when I'm presenting on stage.

PART 3: YOUR CURRENT SKILLS=

List the skills you have built so far - both Hard (technical) and soft people/communication).

What do people often ask for your help with?

Hard Skills:

1. Oracle DBA
2. Shell Scripting
3. Toad Tool support

Soft Skills:

1. Create a Presentation
2. Organize events in the office
3. Drive Wellness initiatives

PART 4: CAUSES OR IMPACTS THAT MATTER TO YOU

Write down what kind of real-world change, industry, or problem you would love to help solve.

What breaks your heart or fires you up?

Examples are mental health for Gen Z, climate action, design for social good, and accessible education.

1. Office Politics (Although it helps you to protect yourself from Corporate Drama, sometimes)
2. Unrealistic commitment to clients
3. Force to deliver things for Tech that you are unfamiliar with.

PART 5: CONNECTING THE DOTS

Now, map the overlaps between your:

1. Interests - People Management and Leading
2. Skills - Communication, Leadership, Automation, DB Administration
3. Energy zones – People, Leadership, and Administration
4. Impact goals - Deliver the project on time and with quality

PART 6: MINI PURPOSE PROJECTS

List 2-3 small project ideas where you can test this overlap.

What can you do this month that combines interest, skill + value?

Examples: Start a blog explaining tech to beginners- Create visuals that simplify complex topics- Volunteer your design skills for a cause you care about

PART 7: WHO BENEFITS FROM THIS?

Write down who your project or purpose could help. Be specific.

If I do this work, it could help-

1. [Group or audience] - Share Knowledge Monthly with Team
2. [Problem it solves] - Resolve the DB Performance problem by fixing instance parameters
3. [Value it creates] - Automated DB refresh process and effort saved from 4 hours to 30 minutes.

REFLECTION

What excites you about this process?

What fears or doubts came up?

What's one small action you can take this week to move toward alignment?

FINDING YOUR NICHE

Open-source, DevOps, Cybersecurity, Cloud Tech, Network, Tech-for-good:

In the chaotic glow of Metroplex, Dhruv "D" Carter was riding high. His startup, *VibeSync*, was the talk of the town, and his slow hustle ethos had Gen Z calling him a vibe curator.

However, something was off.

D's days were packed—coding, pitching, posting—but his heart wasn't in it like before.

The spark of Passion that once lit up his hustle was flickering.

"Am I just grinding for the clout?" he wondered, staring at his RGB-lit setup.

That's when Sage, his mentor, dropped a truth bomb over matcha at Pixel Café.

"Passion is a spark, D. It starts the fire, but purpose keeps it burning."

D blinked, confused. "Isn't Passion enough? I'm out here coding apps and flexing balance."

Sage shook her head. "Passion is fleeting, like a viral YouTube.

Purpose is the why?—the fire that makes your work mean something.

Without it, you are just a hamster on a neon wheel."

She slid him a new challenge: *Find your Purpose in tech. Align your skills with a cause that slaps harder than a trending sound. One month, no excuses.*

D took the bait, not because he was sold, but because Sage's challenges had not steered him wrong yet.

This time, it was not about coding faster or chilling harder—it was about making his hustle matter. The tech world was vast, and D was about to discover that Purpose was not just a buzzword but the ultimate hack for a life that popped off.

Passion gets you started, but Purpose keeps you slaying—find your *why,* or you are just flexing for the algorithm.

The Difference Between Passion and Purpose

Passion is the hype track that gets you moving—coding your first app, debugging at 3 AM, or vibing with a new framework.

The emotional fuel ignites your journey in tech, inspiring you to take the first step and keep going when the going gets tough.

It is emotional, raw, and fleeting. Purpose, though, is the basis that holds it all together. You keep grinding when the hype fades, tying your work to something bigger than yourself.

In tech, **Passion might make you a coder or solution provider. Purpose makes you a game-changer.**

Consider **Lina K**, a Gen Z techie who loved hacking APIs. Her Passion was building sleek apps, but she felt empty churning out e-commerce platforms.

Then she stumbled on *tech-for-good*—using tech to solve real-world problems. Lina pivoted to open-source projects for disaster relief, coding apps that mapped safe routes during floods.

Her Passion sparked the skills; her Purpose—saving lives—kept her coding through sleepless nights. Today, her work powers NGOs.

Quick Stats: *A 2023 Deloitte survey found that 84% of Gen Z want jobs with social impact, and 67% say Purpose drives their career choices over pay.*

Passion is incredible, but Purpose is the fire that fuels long-term W's.

Without it, you are just another dev burning out on CRUD apps for faceless corps.

One example is Kunal Shah, founder of FreeCharge and CRED. He started as a passionate coder but found his Purpose in simplifying digital payments for India's masses. His why—financial inclusion—turned him into a fintech legend, not just a guy who codes.

Simple Hack for Gen Z: Journal your *why?*

Ask: "What problem makes me rage or hype?" Please write it down, no filter.

That is your purpose seed.

Plant it in your tech hustle. See, Passion is the playlist.

Purpose is the Anthem—pick a cause that slaps, or you are just coding for clout.

Real-World IT Needs

Tech is a galaxy of opportunities, but not every star's worth chasing.

Aligning your interests with real-world IT needs means finding where your skills and the world's problems vibe. D loved coding and gaming but was not about to waste his life on another loot-box-ridden mobile game. He needed a niche that matched his energy and made a dent.

The IT world is screaming for talent in specific areas

- **Open-Source**: Free, collaborative projects like Linux or Mozilla need coders to keep the internet democratic. It's lowkey but high-impact.

- **DevOps**: Companies like Netflix and Amazon run on seamless pipelines. DevOps pros are the wizards who keep servers from meeting themselves.

- **Cybersecurity**: With 3.5 million unfilled cyber jobs (per Cybersecurity Ventures, 2023), protecting data is a battlefield where you can be a hero.

- **Tech-for-Good**: From climate tech to healthcare apps, this niche uses code to fix IRL problems, not just pad CEO bonuses.

D's first step was auditing his interests. He geeked out over gaming, anime, and community vibes. Sage pushed him to map these to IT needs.

"Gaming? Look into gamification for education. Anime? AR/VR for storytelling. Community? Open-source or tech-for-good."

D dug into *tech-for-good*, inspired by the stat that 70% of Gen Z want tech to address climate change (Pew Research, 2022). He researched apps that gamified carbon tracking, turning eco-habits into streaks and badges.

Real-World Example: Greta Thunberg's digital allies, like the coders behind *Climate Clock*, built open-source tools to track global warming deadlines. Their interest in activism met IT's need for data-driven advocacy, creating an international movement.

Simple Hack for Gen Z: Make a Venn diagram. One circle - stuff you love (gaming, music, memes). Other circle- IT needs (cybersecurity, AI, open-source).

The overlap? That is your sweet spot. Google one niche and join a Discord community to vibe-check it.

Your interests are your superpower—align them with IT needs, or you are just LARPing as a tech bro.

Finding Your Niche in Tech is the key task

The tech world is a buffet; picking a niche is like choosing your main dish. D was overwhelmed—open-source sounded noble, DevOps paid the bank, cybersecurity was badass, and tech-for-good felt right.

However, finding your niche is crucial. It is about focusing your energy and skills in a direction that aligns with your values and the impact you want to make.

Sage said, "A niche is not just a job; it is your lane. Pick one that matches your skills, values, and the impact you wanna make."

Here is a rundown of hot niches and how to vibe with them

Open-Source: The OG of tech democracy. You contribute to projects like Kubernetes or VS Code, building tools everyone uses. It is unpaid at first, but the clout and skills stack fast.

Example: Neha N started in open-source, contributing to Bitcoin protocols, and now leads MIT's Digital Currency Initiative. *Fit*- This is your jam if you love community and hate gatekeeping.

DevOps: The glue of modern tech. You automate pipelines, scale clouds, and keep apps running smoother than a 60 FPS game.

Example: Kelsey H, a DevOps GOAT, went from sysadmin to Google Cloud evangelist by mastering Kubernetes. *Fit* - DevOps is your vibe if you're a problem-solver who loves efficiency.

Cybersecurity: The digital Wild West. You protect against hackers, ransomware, and data leaks. It's a goldmine with 700,000 new cyber jobs yearly (ISC2, 2023).

Example: Parisa T, Google's "Security Princess," started hacking as a teen and now leads Chrome's security. *Fit*- This is your arena if you're paranoid and love puzzles.

Tech-for-Good: Code with a conscience. You build apps for healthcare, education, or climate action.

Example. **Code.org**, founded by Hadi Partovi, teaches millions to code, leveling the playing field. *Fit.* If you want to save the world while coding, this is your calling.

D leaned toward tech-for-good. His gaming obsession sparked an idea: an app that gamified recycling, rewarding users with virtual skins for real-world eco-actions. He joined an open-source project to test it, collaborating with coders globally.

The community's energy—memes, late-night commits, and shared Purpose—lit him up. He was not just coding. He was building something that mattered.

Real-World Example: Ushahidi, an open-source platform born in Kenya, maps crisis data to save lives during disasters. Coders found Purpose in tech-for-good, turning Passion into global impact.

Simple Hack for Gen Z: Pick one niche and deep-dive for a week. Try a free course (Coursera, edX) or a GitHub project.

Hate it? Pivot. Love it? Double down.

Your niche should feel like a Discord server you never want to leave.

So let us find your tech tribe, or you are just solo-queueing in a game you dislike.

Turning Purpose into Action

Purpose sounds dope, but it is useless without action.

D learned this the hard way when his recycling app idea stalled. He had the *why—fighting* climate change—but no plan.

Sage was not letting him slack.

"Purpose is not a mood board," she said.

"It is a blueprint. Build it, or it is just aesthetic."

D broke it down into steps

1. **Skill Up**: He leveled up his JavaScript and learned APIs for real-time data, using free resources like freeCodeCamp.

2. **Network**: He joined tech-for-good Discords and X threads, connecting with coders and eco-activists.

3. **Prototype**: In two weeks, he built a minimum viable product (MVP) for his app, GreenStreak, and tested it with his squad.

4. **Iterate**: Feedback was brutal but clutch. He tweaked *GreenStreak* to add leaderboards and AR filters, making recycling a flex.

5. **Soft skills**: Communicating the work outcome in email and being present in meetings is essential to ensure your relevance in the team and future growth.

The grind paid off. At a Metroplex pitch fest, D demoed *GreenStreak* to eco-startups and scored a 20K grant. His app went live, and 10K users gamified their recycling in a month. D's Purpose—making sustainability a Gen Z vibe—was now a movement.

Real-World Example: Zipline, a drone delivery startup, uses tech-for-good to deliver medical supplies in Rwanda. Its founders aligned their aerospace passion with global health needs, saving thousands of lives.

Simple Hack for Gen Z: Start small. Pick one project in your niche (e.g., a cybersecurity script, an open-source PR). Ship it in 14 days, no perfectionism. Could you share it on X or GitHub for feedback? Action > vibes.

Remember - *Purpose without a plan is just a Pinterest board—build your why or stay dreaming in 480p.*

Sustaining the Fire

Purpose is not a one-and-done thing. It is a fire you have to tend.

D learned this when *GreenStreak's* growth plateaued.

Users loved it, but scaling was a beast—servers crashed, funding dried up, and D's motivation dipped.

Sage's advice? "Purpose evolves. Keep learning, keep adapting, or your fire's just smoke."

D doubled down on sustainability. He studied cloud scaling for DevOps, joined a cybersecurity bootcamp to secure *GreenStreak*'s data, and contributed to open-source eco-tools.

He also prioritized recovery—meditating, sketching, and muting notifications after 8 PM.

Quick Stat- *A 2024 Gallup study showed 62% of purpose-driven workers avoid burnout by balancing impact with self-care. D was living proof.*

By year's end, *GreenStreak* had 50K users and a partnership with Metroplex's recycling board.

D's Purpose wasn't just personal—it was changing the city. He mentored Nexus kids, teaching them to find *why in* tech.

Remember - *Your purpose is your North Star," he'd say. It is not about the bag. It is about the legacy."*

Real-World Example: **Reshma Saujani**, founder of Girls Who Code, turned her Passion for equity into a purpose-driven movement, teaching 500,000 girls to code. Her fire? Closing the gender gap in tech.

Simple Hack for Gen Z: Schedule a monthly *why* check-in. Ask: "Is my niche still vibing? Am I growing?" Pivot if needed, but never stop learning. Use tools like Notion to track your purpose goals. They tend to your Purpose like a Tamagotchi—feed, grow, or watch it fade to a game-over screen.

Let's look at some useful Hacks

Hack 1: Journal your *why?*. What world problem makes you hype or mad? That is your Purpose. You can also use the Declutter Framework (DFW) Method, as called out in Part I.

Hack 2: Venn diagram your interests (gaming, art) with IT needs (DevOps, cybersecurity). The overlap is your niche. You can also use the CPB method from Part I.

Hack 3: Deep-dive a niche for a week-long course, GitHub, Discord. Vibe-check it.

Hack 4: Ship a small project in 14 days. Share it for feedback. Action > perfection.

Hack 5: Conduct a monthly *"why" check-in.* Track goals, pivot if needed, and keep learning. You can Also Use the CPB method from Part I.

The key epilogue Moral from D's journey was not just a tech glow-up but a masterclass in making it mean something.

Passion is the spark that gets you coding, but Purpose is the fire that keeps you building when the likes fade. Align your interests with IT needs, find a niche that slaps, and turn your *why?* Into action.

The world does not need more grindset zombies.

It needs coders with a cause. So, pick your fire, *Code for clout, or code to change the game.*

Finally, your hustle is only as dope as your *why?*—

Find your Purpose, or you are just spamming commits into the void.

CONCLUSION

To Ignite Your Fire, Keep It Lit. You are made to the end of Passion Is a Spark, Purpose Is the Fire, and if you have been vibing with the journey, you probably feel a mix of hype and overwhelm.

That is real.

Finding your Purpose is not a TikTok trend you can nail in 15 seconds—

It is a slow-burn quest worth every second of the grind.

Let us break down the key lessons from D's story, the Purpose Map, and the worksheets, so you can turn your spark into a fire that does not just glow but *blazes*.

Here is your final roadmap, Gen Z and Alpha fam—point by point, with hacks to practice daily and a punchline to keep you locked in.

Purpose Is Your Why, Not Your Hype

D's journey in Metroplex showed us the difference between Passion and Purpose.

Passion is the hype track that gets you moving, like coding your first app or automating a DB refresh process that saves you hours (shoutout to the worksheet example!).

But Purpose?

The bassline keeps you going when the algorithm stops hyping you up.

Lina K's pivot to tech-for-good and Kunal S's fintech revolution prove it. Passion gets you started, but Purpose makes you a game-changer.

Your Purpose is not just about what lights you up—it is about what keeps you burning when the clout fades.

Ask yourself - *What problem makes me rage or hype?* That is your why?

Practice journaling your why every morning.

Write one sentence, *"Today, I am fired up to [solve this problem/make this impact]."*

Keep it raw, no filter.

The Purpose Map Is Your Compass

The chapter's Purpose Map is your ultimate cheat code. It is a cute diagram and a system for finding your sweet spot.

Let us recap how to use it

Energy: *What makes you feel alive?*

For D, it was gaming and community vibes. For you, it might be presenting on stage or automating challenging tasks (like the DB refresh in the worksheet).

Passion: *What do you care about?* D leaned into climate action; you might vibe with mental health or fighting office politics (as noted in your causes).

Skills: *What are you good at?* D had coding; you have Oracle DBA, shell scripting, and leadership skills (from the worksheet). Do not sleep on soft skills like communication—they are clutch.

Impact: *Who benefits?* D's app helped eco-warriors. Your automated processes saved your team 3.5 hours a day (worksheet win!).

When these overlap, you have found your Purpose. It is not static—it evolves as you grow, just like D's GreenStreak app scaled from an idea to a 50K-user movement.

Remember—your *Purpose lives in the overlap. Do not overthink it— start where you have the strongest vibes and build from there.*

Daily Practice: Pick one Purpose Map element (Energy, Passion, Skills, Impact) to focus on each day.

Example: Monday, list three things that energize you. Tuesday, name a cause you are hyped about. Reflect at night—any overlaps?

Start Small, Win Big

D did not change the world overnight. He started with a small idea—gamifying recycling—and turned it into GreenStreak, which had 10K users in a month.

The worksheet's mini-purpose projects (like sharing knowledge monthly with your team) show how small actions add up.

Purpose does not always shout. Sometimes it whispers in quiet wins, like when your team says, "That DB fix helped."

Remember—you *do not need a viral moment to live your Purpose. Start with a mini project that combines your interests, skills, and impact goals.*

Daily Practice: Spend 10 minutes a day on a mini purpose project.

Example: If you are into people management (worksheet interest), draft a quick team-building idea. If you are about automation, tweak a script to save time: small steps, big W's.

Align Your Hustle with What Matters

The chapter highlighted aligning personal interests with real-world IT needs—open-source, DevOps, cybersecurity, tech-for-good.

D chose tech-for-good because it matched his gaming passion and climate concerns.

You might align your leadership skills with delivering projects on time (worksheet impact goal) or tackle unrealistic client commitments with better communication.

Remember—your interests are your superpower. Map them to a niche that resonates *with the world's needs, or you are just flexing for the algorithm.*

Daily Practice: Google one IT niche (like DevOps or tech-for-good) daily. Join a Discord or X thread about it.

Vibe-check it: *Does this niche light you up?* Could you make an impact here?

Action > Vibes—Build It or Bust

Purpose without action is just a mood board.

D turned his why into GreenStreak by skilling up (JavaScript, APIs), networking (Discords, X threads), and prototyping (MVP in two weeks).

Your worksheet project—automating DB refreshes—saved 3.5 hours daily.

That is the Purpose in action. Zipline's drone deliveries in Rwanda show how aligning Passion with impact can save lives. Do not just dream—do.

Remember - *Ship something small in 14 days. Share it for feedback. Action beats perfection every time.*

Daily Practice: Set a 14-day goal for a purpose project. Break it into daily tasks-

Day 1, brainstorm.

Day 2: learn a skill.

Day 3, draft.

Post your progress on X or GitHub for accountability.

Tend Your Fire—Do not Let It Fade

The purpose is a fire you have to keep lit.

D learned this when GreenStreak plateaued—servers crashed, and motivation dipped.

He doubled down, studied DevOps, joined a cybersecurity boot camp, and prioritized self-care (meditation, sketching).

Quick Stat *-A 2024 Gallup study backs this: 62% of purpose-driven workers avoid burnout with balance.*

Keep learning, keep adapting - Your Purpose will evolve like D's went from an app to mentoring Nexus kids.

Remember*: Schedule a monthly "why" check-in. Is your niche still vibing? Are you growing? Pivot if needed, but never stop fueling your fire.*

Daily Practice: End your day with a quick reflection: "Did I live my Purpose today? What's one thing I learned?" Track your reflection in a Notion doc or journal.

Make It Mean Something—Legacy Over Likes

D's story was not just a tech glow-up.

It was a masterclass in making it meaningful. He did not code for clout—he coded to change Metroplex's recycling game and mentored kids to find out why.

Your purpose projects, like resolving DB performance issues, create value for your team.

The world does not need more grindset zombies. It needs coders, leaders, and creators with a cause.

Remember - *Your hustle is only as dope as your why?. Pick a cause that slaps, or you are just spamming commits for the void.*

Daily Practice: Share one purpose-driven win weekly, big, or small. Tell your team, post on X, or text a friend. Example: "Automated a process today—saved 30 mins for the squad!"

"Write your 'why?' into your work—otherwise, you're just debugging echoes in the algorithm."

– Aalok

Your Purpose is your North Star

Gen Z and Alpha fam. It is not about the bag, the likes, or the clout—it is about the legacy you leave.

The world is waiting for your glow-up, *but you must be **Visible**.*

Chapter 8

DIGITAL VISIBILITY - BUILD IN PUBLIC

"Visibility is currency. Show your work, prove your worth, and let the world pay attention."

– Aalok

Doing great work in silence might sound noble, but silence is invisible in today's digital world.

You could be building the next game-changing app, solving real-world problems with code, or designing interfaces that slap—

However, how will the opportunity find you if no one sees it?

Welcome to the era of building in public.

This concept, popularized by tech communities, encourages individuals to share their work, progress, and learnings openly and consistently. It is not just a trend but a seedling of career opportunities.

Digital visibility is going from "just another dev or designer" to someone noticed, trusted, and respected in the community.

It is about showing your process, not just your polished product, sharing your wins and learning curves, and documenting, not just performing.

People do not just follow perfection—they connect with progress and become part of a larger community.

You do not need to have it all figured out. You need to be real.

A X about a bug you squashed, a GitHub commit on a side project, a short LinkedIn post about what you learned this week—it all stacks up.

And guess what?

That visibility builds credibility.

That credibility brings connections.

And those connections?

They open doors you did not even know existed.

The key is to be authentic because that is what truly resonates with others.

This chapter will explain how to start building in public without the pressure to be perfect.

We are about to discuss the real game—how to use platforms, personal branding, and raw storytelling to your digital advantage.

Not just to get noticed, but to attract the people and opportunities that move your career forward—mentors, collaborators, and doors you did not even know existed.

Because in a scroll-heavy world where everyone is shouting, it is not the loudest who wins—it is the ones who show up with honesty, consistency, and guts.

This is not about hype. It is about *legacy*.

Let us ensure your work does not just flash—*leaves a positive mark.*

The Day I Became a Legend on the IBM Project Floor for a Day

You remember my Day 17 at IBM story; I am fresh off earning some street cred after tackling an Informix assignment like a tech wizard.

I feel like the Tony Stark of databases—minus the suit, but definitely with the ego.

Then, out of nowhere, a wild plot twist.

A senior DBA, the kind of old-timer who probably coded on punch cards, storms onto the floor, asking for *me*.

At the same time, a client escalation lands like a grenade—one of the DBs is throwing tantrums from the app side.

Cue the dramatic music, my anxiety skyrockets faster than a SpaceX rocket.

I am spiraling.

Did I mess up?

What is the escalation number?

Am I getting fired on Day 17?

The hustle kicks in, and my brain is a mess—I am clueless about timelines, and my negative self-talk is louder than a monsoon thunderstorm.

Why am I like this, you ask?

After years of self-analysis, I have dubbed it "3rd Nutty Child Syndrome," a term I use to humorously describe my tendency to take on blame and stress in high-pressure situations.

In my childhood, if anything went wrong in the house—a broken vase, missing snacks, you name it—my name was the first to be yelled.

Usually, I *was* the culprit, but sometimes my elder brother or cousin pulled a sneaky prank, and guess who still got blamed? Yup, me.

So now, when a senior DBA is marching toward my cubicle, I am sweating like I just ran a marathon in flip-flops.

The guys point him at my desk, and my heart rate climbs with every step he takes.

He finally arrives, looking like he is about to drop a bombshell.

"Are you Aalok?" he asks. I nod, shaky, "Yes… is there a problem?"

Long pause.

I blurt out, "Is this about the morning escalation?"

Another long pause—dude, stop with the suspense,

I am dying here! "Oh, no, no," he says, and I am still waiting for the punchline.

Then he drops the bombshell -

"Are you the same person registered on DBA-Village.com?"

I blink. "Uh, yeah, that is me… is there a problem?"

I am expecting a lecture, but instead, he breaks into a grin.

"No problem!

Thank you—Your **Scripts** helped me resolve some DB issues.

And your white papers? Super insightful!"

Then he turns to the floor, announcing to everyone,

"Guys, I have been telling you about this for months. You know, in DBA-Village, He has been sitting right here!"

My jaw drops. The floor erupts—suddenly, I am the "Informix Guy," famous like wildfire.

I went from panic mode to project-floor celebrity in under 60 seconds.

Best. Day. Ever.

Building in public pays off!

Sharing my scripts and white papers on DBA-Village.com was not just about flexing—it created a digital footprint that earned me respect and visibility.

For Gen Z and Alpha readers, please post your work, share your wins, and do not be shy.

Remember—*you never know who is watching—you might just walk up to your cubicle during your next big break!*

Why Build in Public?

Silence is not scaled. Stories do. Be seen or be sorted out.—Aalok

In today's hyper-digital world, building in public is no longer optional—it is the new résumé.

Documenting your learning, failures, micro-wins, and process is not about bragging but building trust and showing where opportunities are born.

Most Gen Zs grew up on Instagram, YouTube, or TikTok. You already know how to "share."

Now it is time to leverage that instinct professionally.

Platforms like GitHub, LinkedIn, and personal blogs are your canvas.

Your tech skills are your tools. Your journey is the content.

Real Talk, not a day goes by that hiring managers, recruiters, founders, and collaborators now look for "proof of work" online. **If you are invisible, you are forgettable.**

GitHub is not just for Code—It is for Career Proof

You do not need to be a senior developer to post. GitHub is most powerful when it reflects your learning curve. Start small:

- Upload your side projects
- Share how you solved a bug
- Commit regularly, even if it is just toy projects

Quick Stat: *According to GitHub's 2023 Oct overview report, 85% of developers feel contributing to public repos boosted their Confidence and career prospects.*

Note Visibility Hack

Star and contribute to trending repos.

Write detailed README files like you are teaching your past self.

Create a pinned repository showcasing your "Tech Garden"—projects, resources, and learnings.

Remember - *GitHub is your coding diary—and the world is watching.*

LinkedIn is not Cringe—It is Underrated AF

Forget the boring résumé PDF.

Today, LinkedIn is your interactive, evolving digital billboard. Post stories, breakdowns, career reflections, or even your weekend bug fix.

It is not about perfection. It is about progress in public.

Quick Stat: *LinkedIn posts with personal stories and practical value receive 7x more engagement than traditional achievement posts (LinkedIn Data, 2024).*

Note Visibility Hack

Engage with comments—every reply is a mini-network expansion

Weekly or Monthly, Wins, fails, or "aha" moments.

Use carousels to simplify tech concepts you are learning.

Remember - *LinkedIn is where opportunities live rent-free.*

Blogs are Legacy Builders

While social media comes and goes, blogs are where you go deep.

They are your long-form thinking—your thought leadership before you even know you have one.

Platform Ideas

- Hashnode and Dev.too Great for early-career devs
- Medium- Popular but competitive—good if you are aiming for tech writing roles
- Personal site (via GitHub Pages or Notion)- Ultimate flex

Quick Stat: *Developers who blog regularly are 33% more likely to get inbound job offers (Stack Overflow Insights, 2022).*

Note Visibility Hack

Write "What I Learned" after every project or bug.

Reflect on struggles- "Why I almost quit CSS (Cascading Style Sheets)" gets more love than "Mastering CSS"?

Link your blog in your LinkedIn bio and GitHub readme.

Remember - *X trend. Blogs live forever.*

Document, Do not Just Create

Perfection kills progress.

Instead of waiting until you are "ready," document what you are doing, trying, failing, or fixing.

You are not writing to Harvard.

You are writing for your tribe—others are just one step behind you.

Micro-Content Ideas

- Code snippets with brief context
- Screenshots of error logs + how you fixed them
- Timeline of your project journey (idea → build → bug → pivot)

Quick Stat: *People who build in public are 12x more likely to get cold DMs from recruiters, mentors, and collaborators (IndieHackers study, 2023).*

Note Visibility Hack

15-sec Loom demo of a project > 1000-word blog.

Schedule "Document Day" weekly—no pressure, post what is happening.

Keep a private Notion, then publish excerpts when ready.

Remember - *You do not need to be an expert. You need to be a note-taker for your future self.*

Confidence Comes From Consistency

Every post, commit, or blog entry is not just visibility—it is proof that you are evolving. When you track your progress publicly, you build a digital mirror.

Over time, you will look back and say, "Wow. I am not who I was."

Quick Stat: *Among developers who post progress online at least once a week, 70% report increased self-belief and community support (Dev.to survey, 2024).*

Note Visibility Hack

Use #100DaysOfCode or #BuildInPublic as habit anchors.

Join and contribute to Discord or Reddit threads in your niche.

Make your milestones visible—do not wait for "the big win"

Remember - *Confidence is not natural. It is practiced in public.*

It is Not About Viral—It is About Value

Chasing virality kills authenticity.

Focus on meaningful visibility.

Your audience is small but mighty: hiring managers, collaborators, mentors, and future you.

Quick Stat: *Just three meaningful professional connections can increase the likelihood of job placement by 60% (LinkedIn Talent Report, 2023).*

Note Visibility Hack

Post helpful tips for the person you were 6 months ago.

Use storytelling: What? Why? How? Wow!

Keep your content skimmable and visual (emojis, bullets, headers).

Remember - *You do not need 10K followers. You need 10 people who care."*

THE VISIBILITY FLYWHEEL: A CAREER GROWTH LOOP

Here is how it compounds

1. *You post progress →*
2. *People engage or learn →*
3. *You gain feedback + visibility →*
4. *You feel validated →*
5. *You build more →*
6. *Opportunities flow in*

It is not linear. It is exponential.

Visual Metaphor - *Build → Document → Share → Feedback → Improve → Repeat → Opportunity.*

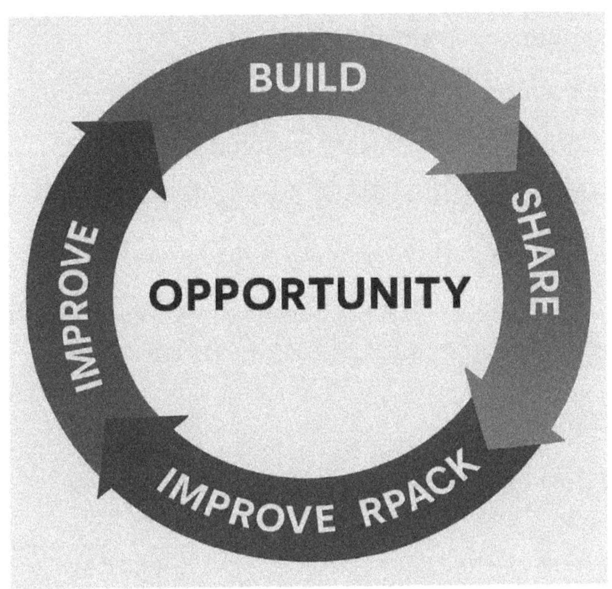

GEN Z SUMMARY—TL;DR WITH HACKS

TL;DR- Success in tech isn't about grinding endlessly—it's about working smart, staying true to your values, and adapting fast.

Stop Waiting, Start Showing

You do not need permission to post.

It is not about waiting but about having the courage to share your messy drafts, tiny wins, and funny fails.

This is your platform, your voice, your power.

Your Platforms

- GitHub = Proof of skill
- LinkedIn = Digital network
- Blogs = Long-term legacy

Top 5 Hacks

1. Weekly "Build Recap" LinkedIn post

2. GitHub readme as your digital CV

3. Start a "Learning In Public" blog on Hashnode

4. Use #buildinpublic and #100daysofcode

5. Pin your best content to LinkedIn highlights.

6. Create a Mind MAP Resume; this is the new trend.

This innovative approach highlights your skills and capabilities in a single view, setting you apart in the digital landscape.

My Recommendation

Be ahead of the curve and create a **Mind Map Resume** –

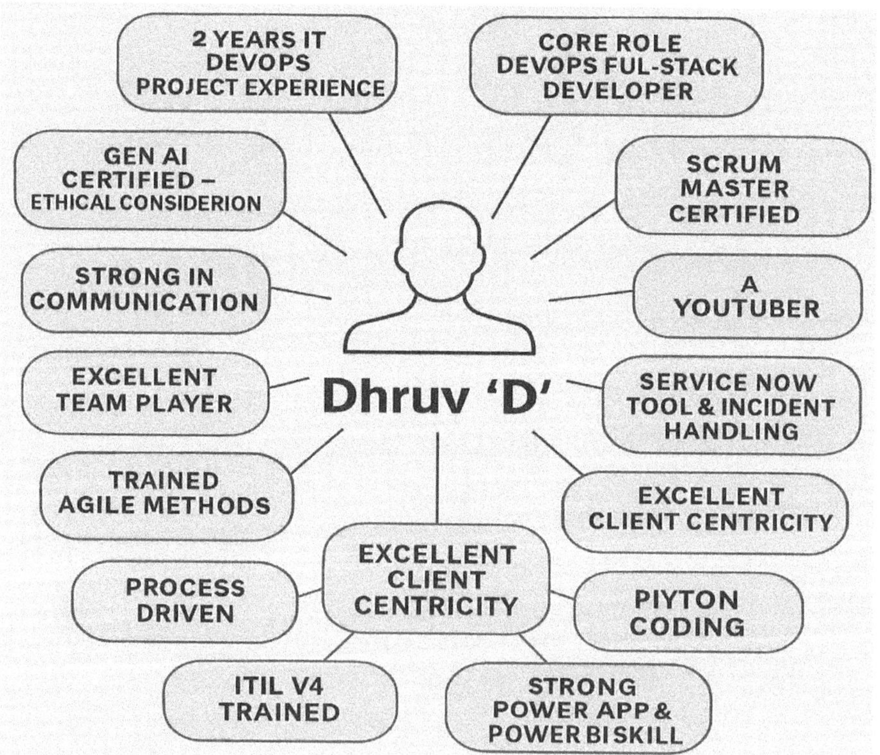

Closing Thought: Visibility is Credibility

You do not need a fancy degree, referral, or job title to win in tech. You need to do your work. That is the new currency of trust.

The world does not reward the most talented. It is the most visible reward.

Remember - *In a noisy world, showing up is your loudest skill.*

Drop the Invisibility Cloak—Your Digital Glow-Up Is Now!

CONCLUSION

Welcome to the final lap of Digital Visibility, be seen or be sorted out," hits harder than a viral TikTok sound.

Let us fan the flames if this chapter has not yet lit a fire under you!

Building in public is not just a trend but your new resume, digital stage, and ticket to opportunities in a hyper-digital world.

The benefits are immense, and the excitement of starting is palpable.

Whether you are a Gen Z coder who grew up on YouTube or an Alpha creator vibin on Discord, you already know how to share—now let us turn that instinct into a career hack.

Let us break it down with key takeaways, a punchline to keep you hyped, and a fire activity that'll have you building in public like a pro, all in a way that slaps for the young generation.

First, let us discuss why sharing your journey is crucial. You are not just coding or designing—crafting a story the world can resonate with.

Your path is unique—when you share it, you light the way for others to walk their own.

In the digital age, being unseen often means being overlooked. Recruiters, managers, and collaborators are not just skimming résumés—they are browsing GitHub, LinkedIn, and blogs for objective evidence of your craft. Showing up online is how you stay on their radar.

Quick Stats - *Back this up: 85% of developers say public repos boosted their careers (GitHub Octoverse, 2023), and developers who blog regularly get 33% more job offers (Stack Overflow, 2022).*

So, post those side projects, share that bug fix, and write that "Why I almost quit CSS" blog.

Your journey—messy drafts, tiny wins, and all—is your content; platforms like GitHub, LinkedIn, and Hashnode are your canvas.

Remember—your *effort is not meant to stay hidden. Show how you work— let the world watch you level up. When you share your journey, you do not just grow—you spark growth in others and draw in the right opportunities.*

Next, let us flip the script to perfection.

You do not need to be a senior developer to build in public— documenting your learning curve is the real flex.

GitHub is not just for code. It is your coding diary (the world's watching).

LinkedIn does not cringe—it is where opportunities live rent-free, with personal posts getting 7x more engagement (LinkedIn Data, 2024).

Blogs on Dev. to or a personal site?

They are your legacy builders, outlasting any X trend.

Document your fails, fixes, and "aha" moments with micro-content like code snippets or 15-sec Loom demos (better than a 1000-word blog!).

People who build in public get 12x more cold DMs from recruiters (IndieHackers, 2023).

Remember - *Do not wait to be "ready"—document weekly, share monthly, and watch your tribe grow.*

Consistency is your secret sauce.

Every commit, post, or blog is a flex on your evolution, building a digital mirror that screams, "I am not who I was." Devs posting weekly report 70% more self-belief (Dev.to, 2024).

The visibility flywheel—Build → Document → Share → Feedback → Improve → Repeat → Opportunity—keeps spinning, landing you collabs and gigs.

Just three meaningful connections can boost job placement by 60% (LinkedIn Talent Report, 2023). Use #100DaysOfCode or #BuildInPublic to stay on track and engage with your community on Discord or Reddit.

Remember - *Consistency > virality. Post small, post often, and watch your confidence stack up like likes.*

Finally, focus on value, not viral.

You do not need 10K followers—just 10 people who care.

Share tips for the person you were six months ago, and use storytelling (What, Why, How, Wow) to keep it skimmable with emojis and visuals.

Pin your best content, star trending repos, and create a mind map resume to flex your skills in one view (it is the new trend!).

My closing thought for this chapter—

"In a noisy world, showing up is your loudest skill"—is your mantra.

Build for value, not clout; opportunities will slide into your Direct Messages (DMs).

Zip it. Build it. Blast it. Alternatively, you are just lagging in the system. – Aalok.

Activity: 7-Day #BuildInPublic Starter Pack - *A 7-day challenge to kickstart your visibility—perfect for Gen Z and Alpha readers who love flexing on socials:*

Day 1: *Pick a small win (a project, a bug fix, a lesson).*

Day 2: *Document it—snap a picture, record a 15-second video, or write a quick post.*

Day 3: *Share it on X, GitHub, or LinkedIn with #BuildInPublic.*

Day 4: *Engage with three people who interact—ask for feedback or hype them up.*

Day 5: *Tweak your work based on feedback (small changes count!).*

Day 6: *Share the updated version—"Here is what I improved, thanks to the squad!"*

Day 7: *Drop a mind map resume displaying your skills (use Canva or Figma) and post it with #BuildInPublic. Tag a friend to join the challenge!*

This activity is your vibe check—share your journey, build your tribe, define Your Own Tech Success, and watch your digital presence glow up!

Chapter 9

DEFINE YOUR TECH SUCCESS

Success is not smooth code—it is the fire you bring when everything breaks, and you still debug forward.

– Aalok

You are probably sipping your morning coffee, scrolling X for the latest tech drops, or tweaking a side hustle buzzing in your head.

However, let us take a beat and ask a question that might shift your perspective.

What does Success in tech mean to you? Not what the algorithm pushes, not what your fam expects, but what makes you feel like a tech legend.

Welcome to Chapter Define Your Own Tech Success, where we are throwing out the old-school playbook—fancy titles, FAANG gigs, or startup clout—and helping you craft a success story as real as your Insta and Facebook for your page.

Because 2025 and beyond, success is not a corporate badge. It is a vibe you build, and Gen Z and Alpha, you are the ones remixing the game.

Let us draw some inspiration from my IBM story. On Day 17 at IBM, a techie faced a make-or-break moment when a senior DBA rolled in. Thanks to his "3rd Nutty Child Syndrome" anxiety, he was sweating bullets.

However, I have been building publicly, sharing my scripts and white papers on DBA-Village.com. If you go ahead and search me 'aalok,' you will find some work from 2003 and 2004 archived on this site.

That digital trail turned him into the "Informix Guy" on the project floor, earning props from the senior DBA and his whole squad. My success was not a corner office—it was respect, visibility, and impact, all because he defined it his way by sharing his journey.

My key learning from my IBM job was that a tech job is about resolving problems. The success of Tech is about resolving business problems.

However, here is the real talk—those might not be your vibe. Perhaps success for you is building an app that benefits your community, as Dhruv "D" Carter did in the previous chapter with GreenStreak, gamifying recycling to make Metroplex greener and attracting 50,000 users. Alternatively, maybe it is freelancing on Upwork, setting your hours while you code for small businesses because freedom is your ultimate flex.

For Gen Z and Alpha, this is your moment.

Quick Stat- *A 2023 Deloitte survey says 84% of you prioritize purpose over pay, so why follow someone else's script?*

This chapter will help you unpack your "why," build a skill stack that slaps and explore paths like freelancing or indie hacking.

Let us define your tech success—your rules, your glow-up!

SUCCESS IS NOT A FILTER—IT IS YOUR VIBE

What Does Tech Success Mean to You?

Success in tech is not a one-size-fits-all Instagram filter—it is a vibe you define.

For some, it is a six-figure dev job. For others, it is coding for a cause or building a YouTube following.

As a Gen Z or Alpha reader, you can rewrite the rules of success on your terms. Embrace this freedom and define your unique path to success.

Why Defining Your Success Matters?

The grind for titles and fat paychecks? It is a trap many fall into.

Chasing traditional success markers like job titles or salaries may look good on paper, but they often come with a hidden cost: burnout.

Quick Stat: *According to Deloitte (2023), 84% of Gen Z would rather pursue purpose than just a paycheck.*

What is more telling?

That is not just a trend—it is a wake-up call.

If you have ever felt that pull to do something that matters in tech, you are not alone.

Redefining success on your terms—where impact > income—is becoming the new normal.

Unpack the Hype—What is Driving You?

- Reflect on Your "Why?"

Ask yourself: Are you chasing clout, passion, impact, or stability?

What makes you feel "on fire" in tech? What problem do you want to solve?

Ditch the Algorithm of Comparison

- Address the trap of comparing yourself to viral tech influencers or senior devs on X.

In previous chapters, Dhruv "D" Carter (from your prior context) thought success was all about startup fame until he found his vibe in tech for good.

ACTIVITY FOR YOU

Create Your Success Mood Board

- Suggest a quick activity - Grab a Notion page or Pinterest board and pin 3-5 things that scream "tech success" to you—
- Maybe a screenshot of an open-source project, a dream company logo, or a cause you care about.

BUILD YOUR SUCCESS BLUEPRINT

Step 1: Identify Your Core Values - Break down how values shape success

Are you about innovation (building new tools), community (open-source collabs), or impact (tech-for-good)?

We have read how Dhruv's pivot to GreenStreak exemplifies aligning with his values.

Step 2: Map Your Skills to Your Goals

- Guide readers to audit their skills (like Dhruv's Web DevOps and Scrum Master experience) and match them to their vision.

- Include a table: one column for skills (e.g., GitHub, Azure) and another for how they tie to goals (e.g., contributing to open-source, landing a cloud gig).

Step 3: Set Your Metrics

- Encourage non-traditional metrics, such as lines of code contributed, people helped, or personal growth (e.g., "I learned APIs this month!").
- Highlight that success can be 10K users on an app or just one "thank you" from a teammate.

Find Your Tech Tribe

Joining Discord servers or X communities in your niche (e.g., #100DaysOfCode) to see how others define success.

It will spark ideas for your path.

AVOID THE BURNOUT TRAP

Balance Impact with Self-Care

During my HP Paris project in the previous chapter, my motivation dipped. I bounced back with a mindset of contributing to the team, even for those unaware of tech skills. (Strategy to look at the big picture, What is the end goal here? What can I do? Where do I need help? Communicate Status Continuously)

The Dhruv's plateau moment with GreenStreak—servers crashed, and motivation dipped. He bounced back with self-care (meditation, sketching) and upskilling (DevOps, cybersecurity).

Quick Stat - *Cite the 2024 Gallup stat: 62% of purpose-driven workers avoid burnout with balance.*

Set Boundaries, Not Limits

Mute notifications after < ___PM> or take "no-code Sundays" to recharge.

Remember - Success is not sustainable, if you are burned out chasing it.

Activity: Schedule a "Why Check-In"

Prompt a monthly reflection – Is my tech path still vibin?

What is one thing I need to tweak? Track it in a Notion doc or journal.

Your Success Flywheel—Keep It Spinning

The Cycle: Build → Reflect → Tweak → Grow

Introduce a successful flywheel similar to the visibility flywheel from prior chapters: Build (work on projects), Reflect (check your metrics), Tweak (pivot if needed), Grow (level up).

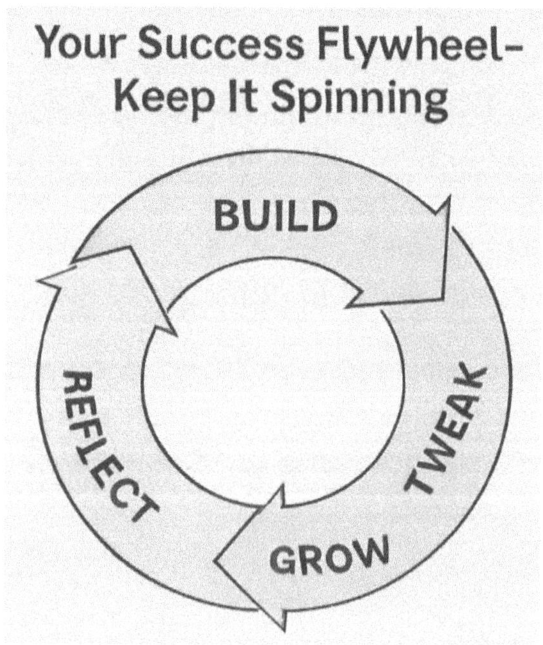

Stay Flexible—Success Evolves

Emphasize that success is not static. Dhruv's definition of success evolved from app downloads to mentoring.

Yours will, too. Encourage embracing pivots as growth, not failure.

Hack: Celebrate Micro-Wins

Suggest sharing micro-wins on X or LinkedIn (e.g., "Just pushed my first commit!") to keep momentum. It is not flexing—it is fueling your flywheel.

Remember - *Own your tech success—build, flex, and remix it until it slaps, because the world needs your unique glow-up!*

Let me share one of my favorite Earl Nightingale's definitions of success, which is one of the most powerful and timeless- ***Success is the progressive realization of a worthy ideal.***"

What does that mean?

Progressive: It is a journey, not a destination. You do not have to "arrive" to succeed—you must keep moving toward your goal.

Realization: You are actively turning your vision into reality.

Worthy ideal: Something meaningful to you, not what society says is success.

In simpler understanding

You are already successful if you know what you want and are actively working toward it daily.

This definition shifts success from being about titles, money, or fame to **personal purpose and progress.**

It is especially relevant in today's fast-changing tech and hustle culture.

Want a punchy modern remix of it for your book or a post?

Remember—success is not a destination with Wi-Fi and stock options. It is the daily decision to build what sets your soul on fire. Perfection slows you down, while purpose *keeps you going.*

CONCLUSION

Your Tech Success, Your Rules, Your Definition.

While we are wrapping up with a straight-fire vibe, Gen Z and Alpha fam!

You have just vibed through *Define Your Own Tech Success,* and if Dhruv "D" Carter's journey with GreenStreak or Lina K's tech-for-good pivot did not spark some serious inspo, let us crank up the heat.

This chapter was not about copying someone else's glow-up but coding your own.

Whether you are freelancing on Fiverr, building a SaaS as an indie hacker, or just flexing your first GitHub commit, success in tech is not a corporate checklist. It is a remix you drop on your terms, and you are the DJ of your tech journey.

Let us break it down with takeaways that slap, a punchline that sticks, and a vibe that'll have you ready to own the digital stage.

First, let us discuss owning your *"why?"*

Success is not about what looks good on LinkedIn but what makes you feel alive.

Quick Stat- *84% of Gen Z prioritize purpose over pay (Deloitte, 2023). So, stop chasing someone else's algorithm and start chasing what lights you up.*

Remember—*your "why?" is your Wi-Fi—stay connected to it, and you will never lose signal.*

Next, let us ditch the titles and flex your path. You do not need "Senior Dev" on your badge to win. Freelancers are out here setting their hours on Upwork, solopreneurs are building apps like Dhruv did, and indie hackers are creating micro-SaaS tools that pop off on IndieHackers.com.

Success can be 100 commits, helping one person with your code, or just learning a new skill. It is your metrics, your rules. Dhruv's success was not a paycheck but mentoring Nexus kids and changing his city.

The key learning titles are overrated—*build your tech empire.*

Moreover, do not let procrastination kill your vibe.

We dropped a 5-minute timer hack to beat it, start small, reward yourself, and reflect daily.

Lina K coded through sleepless nights for disaster relief because she believed in her "why?"—you can too.

Your success flywheel—Build → Reflect → Tweak → Grow—keeps spinning as long as you keep showing up.

Share your micro-wins on X with #DefineTechSuccess, like "Just pushed my first commit—vibes only!"

Remember - *Small steps + big vibes = a success flywheel that never stops.*

Here is the truth: The tech world does not care about your degree or your follower count—it rewards the ones who show up, mess, and keep bouncing back, being resilient.

Whether you are posting your journey on GitHub, sharing a "What I Learned" blog on Hashnode, or just flexing a mind map resume (yep, that is the new wave!), You are already winning by being visible.

Success is not a straight line—it is a loop, and every step you take makes you a better coder, creator, or collaborator.

So, Gen Z and Alpha fam, let us make the tech world your playground.

Define your vibe, build your path, and watch your glow-up go viral in all the ways that matter.

Remember - *Success is not a download—it is a vibe you code, so drop the beat!*

Tech success is not a corporate checklist—it is your vibe, *Your Rules!*

Whether coding for climate, mastering Azure, or teaching others on YouTube, you can decide what "winning" looks like.

Activity for you

Share Your Success Vibe - Invite readers to post their definition of success on X with #DefineTechSuccess.

THE CONCLUSION - THE MAP IS YOUR MIND

You are not just in the game. You are designing the rules. Your MIND is the MAP.

– Aalok

All young generations, Gen-Z and Gen Alpha are stuck in a mental traffic jam due to "Fried Dopamine," which we have understood in our welcome to the digital hustle chapter, as a result of social media overdose.

YOUR UNCONTROLLABLE SELF-TALK IS YOUR TRAFFIC JAM

However, in between, there is a soft honking of souls who try to bring our attention to the present for a better immediate future.

Those who listen quickly, who can calm down, and start using common sense to move from ordinary emotional intelligence to happiness

Let us understand this with a small story- *"Stuck in a Jam, but the Soul has Got a Horn"*

So there you are, scrolling. Facebook, Insta, Snap, YouTube Shorts—your thumb has more mileage than your sneakers.

You started watching a cat doing yoga, and suddenly it is 2 AM, and you're watching a dude deep-fry his iPhone in a bathtub full of cheese. Classic.

Welcome to the mental traffic jam, brought to you by none other than—drumroll—Fried Dopamine.

That is right. Your brain is a pleasure center, lit like Coachella, but guess what?

You are not going anywhere. You are emotionally parked in neutral, your mind revving like a Lambo with no tires.

See, the problem is not social media alone. It is the overdose.

You have taken so many quick dopamine hits that real life feels like a boring group project.

Washing dishes? Lame. Talking to Grandma? Meh. Homework? HAHA.

Moreover, here is the twist – it is not just your brain that's stuck.

It is your self-talk. That voice in your head? It is in full road-rage mode.

"I am not good enough," "Everyone is ahead," - *Why don't I look like that influencer who lives in Bali and drinks oat milk lattes all day?* Beep beep—that is your self-doubt merging without a blinker.

However, wait… listen closely.

Underneath all the chaos, there is a soft honk. It is not a car alarm, not the screeching brakes of anxiety.

No, it is your soul.

Yeah, it has been trying to get your attention this whole time. Real chill. Not dramatic.

Just a friendly "Hey… remember me?"

Your soul does not scream—it whispers.

It nudges you when you are doomscrolling and suddenly feel empty. It taps your shoulder when lying in bed, wondering if there is more to life than Wi-Fi and likes.

It gently suggests, "Maybe just... pause? Breathe? Touch some grass?"

Moreover, here is the kicker - those who listen to that soft honk?

They start moving.

Not physically (unless it is toward a therapist or an actual tree), but emotionally.

They shift lanes—from emotional confusion to emotional intelligence, brain fog to common sense.

From "why me?" to "what now?"

It is like clearing the jam one car at a time. You realize your worth is not in your follower count, glow-up, or ability to go viral. You can pause, reboot, and live fully present.

Because the moment you stop racing other people's highlight reels and start driving your inner GPS, you find something wild—happiness.

Not that temporary, junk-food kind. However, the deep, satisfying, "dang, I am okay" kind.

So next time you feel stuck, remember - the jam is not forever.

The soul is still honking, softly but steadily.

All you have to do?

Roll the window down. And listen.

Now go on—unclog that mind. The road to joy is waiting.

Moreover, it has **no traffic**.

This final chapter should feel like a culmination—powerful, reflective, and empowering.

The message in this section blends practical, personal, and philosophical elements, delivering a final push for Gen Z/Alpha readers to take full ownership of their tech career journey and not follow someone else's roadmap.

Your path is not predetermined.

You have the power to design your path.

You are the Architect.

You are the Engine.

Your Mind is a MAP.

You are standing at the edge of the "career jungle."

You are not here to follow a roadmap.

You are here to build one, unique to your skills, interests, and aspirations.

You do not need permission to lead.

You need direction—and the guts to draw your damn MAP.

This freedom is your strength.

There is no clean trail. No glowing sign that reads **"This Way to Success."**

There are a few footprints, some worn-out advice, maybe a YouTube guru yelling at you to "GRIND 24/7." However, no one—not your college, job, or algorithm—can tell you where your path leads.

LET US KILL THE MYTH RIGHT NOW

You do not need a fancy title to start your tech career.

You need not be "Senior Anything" to ship something real.

You do not need a big-name company on your resume to make a real impact.

What do you need? Ownership. Direction. Momentum.

That is your job now.

The career ladder is obsolete—built for climbing someone else's dream. Design a playground where you explore, experiment, and evolve. Ladders break. Playgrounds grow. And guess what? You are the architect with the blueprint. – Aalok

We were told to climb a ladder. However, ladders are rigid.

They are linear. And *honestly?* Boring.

In today's tech world, careers look more like obstacle courses. Or skate parks. Or open-world games. You can pivot from Dev to UX.

You can go from freelancing to founding. You can be a YouTuber, a backend engineer, and a community educator in the same month.

THE SELF-MADE BLUEPRINT

From Identity Crisis to Identity Design:

You do not start with a title—you start with a taste. You try, you fail, you tinker, you ship.

You are not a "full stack dev" yet? Who cares.

You have never managed a team? You can still lead yourself.

You did not go to MIT? Your GitHub is your diploma –

Remember - *Clarity comes from execution, not overthinking.*

HERE IS HOW REAL SELF-MADE IT PROS START

- They build before they are ready.

- They ship projects before they are perfect.
- They create digital proof before the job offers.

BUILD YOUR MIND MAP RESUME – *WE WILL SOON DIVE INTO YOUR MIND MAP*

- Mindset → your mental operating system
- Intentionality → choosing your direction daily
- Navigation → adaptability as a muscle
- Discipline → slow hustle over shiny objects

Forget job titles. Start building a resume that no one can take away. Because what have you built, learned, or explored that shows who you are, beyond your job title?" Could you write it down? That is your foundation.

Remember—anyone *can fake a title. However, you cannot fake your mindset, growth, or drive. Your personal growth is the real currency in the tech industry.*

WHAT IF YOUR MOST POWERFUL RESUME IS NOT ON PAPER, BUT IN YOUR HEAD?

A New Career DNA for IT Pros

Let us get one thing straight.

Your job title is not your identity. It is a temporary label, like a sticky note on your forehead during a party game.

The real stuff—the substance that makes you stand out—is under the hood.

In this digital hustle era, we need a new kind of resume.

One that goes beyond bullet points and buzzwords. A resume that reflects:

- *How do you think?*
- *How do you adapt?*
- *What drives you?*
- *And how consistently you show up.*

Now let us enter into the MIND MAP Resume

This is not just a clever acronym. It is your internal GPS for designing a resilient, creative, self-made IT career.

M = MINDSET → YOUR CAREER'S OPERATING SYSTEM

Your mindset shapes how you react to challenges, learn from failures, and handle impostor syndrome, which is part of the IT onboarding process.

Do you panic when things break? Or do you get curious and debug your way out?

Remember: *Skills can be taught. Titles can be given. But mindset? That is self-installed.*

I = INTENTIONALITY → Not Just Busy. Aligned

Everyone is hustling. However, not everyone is aligning. Intentionality is about making deliberate moves, not random scrolls.

Think of it this way - Posting on LinkedIn often does not matter if your content lacks soul. Applying for 50 jobs will not help if you have not reflected on what excites you.

Intentional tech professionals

- Choose what they learn based on future trends,
- Document their process to build visibility,
- And say no to noise so they can say yes to growth.

  Try the "3-2-1 Weekly Review":

- *3 things you learned,*
- *2 things you built,*
- *1 thing you will double down on next week.*

Remember - *The algorithm loves consistency. However, success loves clarity.*

N = NAVIGATION → Adapt Fast, Learn Smart

The only constant in tech?

Change. Will React become obsolete? You learn Svelte. Twitter becomes X? You pivot to Threads.

Your internship gets canceled? You launch a personal API project.

Adaptability is not a buzzword anymore—it is a non-negotiable career.

World Fluency

- Utilize AI tools to accelerate your learning, such as ChatGPT for problem-solving and GitHub Copilot for prototyping.
- Explore cross-functional collaborations - a developer working with design or a data analyst building dashboards for business teams.

Remember – *You are not just a coder. You are a career navigator.*

D = DISCIPLINE → SHOW UP WHEN IT IS BORING

Discipline is underrated in a world obsessed with dopamine.

No one is clapping while you are

- *debug CSS,*
- *Rewrite the README files,*
- *Or send your 9th cold email.*

However, here is the truth: Those quiet, unsexy moments?

They are compounding your future. Skills do not grow in chaos.

It grows in consistency. You do not need to be extreme. You need to be steady.

Try the "Slow Hustle Mode"

- *1 hour/day of focused work,*
- *1 post/week showing your progress,*
- *1 deep reflection/month on what is working.*

Remember: *Motivation fades—discipline ships.*

What does a MIND MAP Resume Look Like?

It is not a PDF or a Canva template. It is how you think, act, evolve, and publicly document your career.

Here is how to write your own:

MIND = **M** - Internal World + **I** - Focus + **N** - Agility + **D**-Consistency

MIND (Internal World)

- Journal 1x/week about what is challenging you and how you are responding.
- Note the mindset shifts you have made recently.

INTENTIONALITY (Focus)

- List three goals for the month and align all your content or projects around them.

NAVIGATION (Agility)

- Track what new tools or trends you are exploring.
- Review how fast you pivoted when priorities changed.

DISCIPLINE (Consistency)

Build a ritual tracker. Not for perfection, but for **proof of persistence**

Example: Dhruv 'D' MIND MAP Tracker (Age 22, Backend DevOps → DevRel)

- **M:** Learned to reframe "failure" as a feature request for his life.
- **I:** Focused 3 months on content + community engagement vs chasing every hackathon.
- **N:** Pivoted to public speaking by joining X Spaces and LinkedIn Lives.

D: Showed up 5 days/week with GitHub commits + 1 long-form blog every month

Summary Hack: For the Gen Z / Alpha IT Hustler

- **MINDSET**: Install the upgrade. Default settings won't get you far.
- **INTENTIONALITY**: No more "spray and pray." Focus beats frenzy.
- **NAVIGATION**: If it's shifting, so should you. Stay nimble.
- **DISCIPLINE**: Hustle quietly, show results loudly.

Remember - *You already have a resume. It is every decision you have made when no one was watching.*

Your mindset - *Not the "manifest it" kind. The real kind. The one that decides whether you bounce back or burn out. Whether you blame the bug or debug your blind spot.*

This is not fluff. It is your career firmware.

Quick Stat: *According to Stanford psychologist Carol Dweck, students and professionals with a growth mindset outperform fixed-mindset peers by over **40%** in long-term goal execution and learning adaptation.*

Remember – *Your skills can be elite. But your progress will lag if your head isn't in the game.*

Mind Your MIND MAP (Operating System)

Your career is not built on downloads.

It is built on daily uploads to your potential.

All right, you have now got the blueprint for MINDSET. ADAPTABILITY. PURPOSE.

However, here is the final boss level most do not talk about…

None of this works without practice—real, repeatable, daily reps. Like code becomes a product when shipped, self-growth becomes results when it is integrated into your system.

MAP File—a library of digital drills, tools, habits, and hacks to install your new operating system, which we have learn in 3 parts in this book.

Think of it like your own custom productivity stack for becoming

- **Mindset** - *More self-aware*
- **Adaptability** - *More flexible and future-proof*
- **Purpose** - *More grounded and driven*

MINDSET Practice Hacks - Tools to Reboot Your Inner OS When Self-Doubt, Stress, or Burnout Creeps In.

The Debug Your Inner Voice Template

Whenever imposter syndrome hits, write a Thought: "I am not qualified for this."

Do the reality check each time: "I have built _____, learned _____, and asked for feedback _____ times."

Mind Input is *"I am in debug mode, not failure mode."*

Remember - *If your code does not run the first time, you do not quit—you fix the bug. Do the same with your thoughts.*

MVP Morning Log (5 min journal)

Open a blank doc or app like Notion. Every morning:

- Mental Mode Today: (focused/scattered / anxious/excited?)
- One small mindset I am testing:
- What I will say "no" to today:
- One thing I will do to grow 1% today:

Weekly Reflection (The "Git Log" of You)

Just like you commit code, commit a self-update every Friday or Weekend-

- *Wins:*
- *Bugs in mindset:*
- *Lessons:*
- *Reframe, I will try next week:*

ADAPTABILITY Practice Hacks - Tactics to flex, stretch, and level up fast without burnout

The "2x2 Stretch Grid"

Every month, rate your current work on:

	Confident	*Learning Curve*
Core Role	*(eg. React dev)*	*(eg. DevOps basics)*
Side Skills	*(eg. writing docs)*	*(eg. public speaking)*

Focus on ONE area each month. Use it as your adaptability sprint.

The Learning Hour Block

Schedule 2 hours/week for unstructured learning:

- One YouTube tutorial,
- One blog deep dive
- One GitHub repo to explore

Tools: Zotero for saving learning references, Tana or Notion for organizing notes.

Note: Trust me, this will work like fresh Oxygen.

Project Flip Drill

Once a month, take a project and reimagine it:

- "What if this had to be done with no code?"
- "What if I had to explain this to a 10-year-old?"
- "What would happen if the user were blind?"

Remember – *Adaptability is not about knowing everything. It is about asking better questions, faster.*

Mindset Shifts for Adaptability in Tech Careers

From	To
"I need to be ready before I start."	"I will start, then get ready along the way."
"This is not what I studied."	"This is a chance to expand my skillset."
"I failed—maybe I am not cut out for this."	"That is data. Let me reroute and try again."
"I only do backend/frontend/data/etc."	"I am a problem-solver first, specialist second."

(Condt.)

From	To
"My plan is not working."	"Time to switch lanes, not quit the race."
"I am behind."	"Everyone has a different loading bar."

PURPOSE Practice Hacks - Stay aligned with your "why" even when the grind hits hard

The Purpose Check-in - Once a quarter, revisit these three prompts:

- Do I still believe in the mission of what I am working on?

- What work felt most aligned with my values lately?

- What do I want more/less of in my day-to-day role?

If your answers feel off, do not panic—pivot your approach over the next 30 days.

"Purpose Pulse" Projects - Keep a tiny side project alive that:

- Solves a real problem you care about

- Might not scale—but feels real and energizing

- Is build-in-public ready (for LinkedIn, GitHub, or a personal blog)

Examples

- A mental health check-in bot for your community

- A dev blog series for non-native English speakers

- A landing page generator for indie creators

Note: These often become your most hireable assets.

Purpose People Tracker

Create a list of 10 people whose work aligns with your purpose.

- Follow them on LinkedIn/Twitter
- Engage with their posts
- Reach out quarterly with thoughtful questions
- Build relational, not transactional, networks

Note: Readwise + Mailbrew to keep track of their content and quotes

Remember - *You can borrow someone's career path, but you cannot borrow their purpose.*

Summary Hack: For the Gen Z / Alpha Hustler

- Mindset is not optional. It is oxygen.
- Replace comparison with curiosity.
- Do not aim for approval. Aim for growth.
- Fail publicly. Recover visibly. Learn relentlessly.

Remember: *Your mindset is the only tool you'll use in every project, pivot, and pitch. Master it early and upgrade it often.*

Success is your Operating System. You build it. You run it. You fly it."

— **Aalok**

This means you control your success. You have the power to build it, run it, and take it to new heights.

The Call to Action—Time to Hit "Go"

You have made it through the hard stuff. You have built the structure of your **MIND MAP**.

You have learned how to cultivate mindset, adaptability, and purpose as tools in your startup.

Here is what ties it all together: **It is your turn to ship this.**

No one is coming to save you. However, that is the best news because the road is yours to carve when driving.

Here is your closing assignment, but first: **No more excuses.**

This is not just a chapter to close and forget. **This is your startup moment.**

Revisit Your MAP—Write it down. Map out your mindset. Next, choose an adaptable skill to level up. *Align it with your purpose. Make it visible.*

Ship Your First Project – *No, not the perfect one. The **imperfect** one that gets you started. You have no more room for procrastination.*

Build in Public – *Share what you are learning. Post a project on GitHub. Write about your journey on LinkedIn. Be bold in showing your evolution.*

Tweak Your Engine Every 30 Days – *Check your MAP every month. Reflect on what is working, what needs a new approach, and where you can go next. Iterate.*

Minor updates are better than waiting for the "big moment." Just like you can keep pushing code to production, keep pushing yourself.

One commit at a time

Remember - *Do not just code for the clout—hack your MIND MAP, architect your saga, and engineer a future that crashes the servers of mediocrity.*

Be Proud You Are the Future of IT

Right now, someone is looking at the path you are about to walk and thinking- That is impossible. That is too big of a dream, and they see you. You, the one who is:

- Resilient when things break
- Adaptable when technologies shift

- Purpose-driven, making an impact that goes beyond just a paycheck

You are proof that this is the future of IT.

You are the one who paves the way for what comes next.

What is Next for You: The World Needs You to Build, Lead, and Create

You are not just building a career. As you step into this world of possibilities, remember that.

You are not just building a career.

You are shaping Your Future.

You are building a legacy—a testament to your impact on the future of IT.

With the right tools at your fingertips and a world of digital opportunities ahead, your success story is yours to write.

Just remember—real IT pros do not chase trends.

They *start* them. They do not just follow the map—they draw their own.

They are the ones who **set them and shape the industry's future**.

And **you?** You have got the power to do precisely that.

So, here is my last word –

Do not just build the life you can make; build the life you will build. Moreover, do it with curiosity, passion, purpose, and Style.

Finally, as promised in Part I, Chapter 2, I'm sharing the Secret Technique

The Single Secret Technique (SSt) is a powerful tool that empowers you to take control of your mindset and self-talk.

After reading all the sections in this book and practicing the tips and tricks that resonate with you, if you feel overwhelmed or unable to resolve your procrastination problem, try (SSt) as a rescue.

Disclaimer: Remember, the problem is not the method or frameworks, but rather, most of the time, it is our self-talk, self-doubt, or procrastination issues.

My recommendation? Start creating your MAP, and if there are breaks in your rituals that disrupt your routine, use SSt to transition back smoothly.

Why is It Called the Single Secret Technique?

Because at the core of every productivity hack, time-block method, or motivational framework. There is just one true gatekeeper: *your inner dialogue*—your self-talk.

The Single Secret Technique (SST) isn't a trendy method or a fancy productivity system.

It's a *quiet override button* for when routines fail, Hustle gets noisy, or motivation dips.

Why is it "single"?

No matter the situation—burnout, distraction, or confusion—it all begins and ends with how you speak to yourself.

Why "secret"?

Because we often overlook the simplest things.

Silence. A mental trigger. A 10-second reflection.

They seem too small to matter—until they *reset your rhythm, sharpen your focus*, and *bring you back to life*.

These micro-techniques are your mental pit stops, your bounce-back rituals.

They do not rely on motivation, and they *reboot it.*

The SSt works not because it's complicated, but because it's deeply personal.

It aligns your mind, actions, and energy—quickly.

Oh yes! It has been tested on me over many years. Here are the SSt for you to ponder and practice to bounce back:

SST One: *Silence & Breath Reset*

Close your eyes and observe just one minute of silence while switching between complex tasks. Count your breaths 21 times.

This gives a break to present Hustle and quickly prepares your mind for the next task, allowing you to be productive.

SST Two: *Memory Trigger*

To sharpen your memory, install a trigger point in your mind. For example, if you buy something at a shop, start from home. Plant the number '10' in your mind, which your brain will recall when you enter the shop. If you can recall, you are naturally proud of yourself, and can tap into your subconscious mind. If not, do not worry; it will come with some practice. This technique helped me become effective in managing my self-talk.

Disclaimer: Although it requires considerable practice, it is a powerful technique.

SST Three: *Self-Check Reflection*

At the end of each day, ask yourself, "How am I doing?" If the answer is "Good" or "OK," quickly look at things you liked about today. If the answer is "No," then promptly review the situations and circumstances in your control and outside of your control to ponder.

You do not need to find a solution for the cause; it will come naturally to you. Conduct this daily self-reflection practice automatically; it helps build resilience to bounce back.

The Single Secret Technique (SST) helps you bounce back by managing self-talk and routines. Utilize silence, memory triggers, and daily reflection to cultivate resilience.

You have the MIND MAP—Mindset to believe, adaptability to pivot, and purpose to make it mean something.

You are the architect, designing a journey that is unapologetically yours. You are the engine, powering it with discipline, community, and balance.

Gen Z and Alpha, you are not here to debug someone else's code—you are here to hack the matrix, rewrite reality, and build an IT legacy that slaps harder than a viral X thread.

The hacks are in your toolkit, your case studies are your inspo (inspiration), and the future is your repo (Reputation).

So, grab your keyboard, push your first commit today, and own your journey.

The M A P is Yours, And Your Sharp MIND Power is UNSTOPPABLE.

REFERENCES

"Exploring Undergraduate Student Perceptions of Career Readiness: A Survey" by Cristen M. D'Accordo. https://digitalcommons.molloy.edu/etd/200/

ENGLISH - Thank you for helping me grow! Foldable, colorable card | Made By Teachers. https://www.madebyteachers.com/products/english-thank-you-for-helping-me-grow-foldable-colorable-card/

Strategies for Overcoming Learning Challenges in the Workplace - Abakada Studios. https://www.abakadastudios.com/technology/strategies-for-overcoming-learning-challenges-in-the-workplace/

Driving Traffic to Your Affiliate Offers: Social Media Success. https://www.digitalanfal.com/driving-traffic-to-your-affiliate-offers-strategies-for-social-media-success/

Is upskilling a necessity or luxury? https://employsure.co.nz/blog/upskilling-employees-for-small-businesses

Rain of Rewards - From Sand to Field: A Center-Back's Dream - WebNovel. https://en.webnovel.com/book/31058583700815205/83500209803418735

Addressing The Digital Skills Gap: Strategies For Success. https://welovesalt.com/news/hiring-advice/map-digital-skills-gap/

Hiring Trends Index: a look at the recruitment landscape of Q1 2024 | Totaljobs. https://www.totaljobs.com/recruiter-advice/hiring-trends-index-a-look-at-the-recruitment-landscape-of-q1-2024

Custom Microlearning Course Development Services. https://www.msnod.com/microlearning-development-services.html

Importance of Taking Breaks: Why Rest is Productive - Student Navigator. https://studentnavigator.blog/importance-of-taking-breaks-why-rest-is-productive/?v=4a213ca45f68

Maximising Efficiency: Lessons in Productivity from Business Experts. https://inspirepreneurmagazine.com/maximising-efficiency-lessons-in-productivity-from-business-experts/

Set a 6-Minute Timer for Maximum Efficiency. https://www.aurahealth.io:443/blog/set-a-6-minute-timer-for-maximum-efficiency

Healthy Habits for Energy | Blog - Patch Brand – The Patch Brand. https://thepatchbrand.com/blogs/living-healthier-1/healthy-habits-for-energy

Importance of Taking Breaks: Why Rest is Productive - Student Navigator. https://studentnavigator.blog/importance-of-taking-breaks-why-rest-is-productive/?v=4a213ca45f68

3 Quick and Easy Instagram Marketing Tips for Busy Soulpreneurs - Erin MacCoy Coaching. https://erinmaccoycoaching.com/3-quick-and-easy-instagram-marketing-tips-for-busy-soulpreneurs/

Impulsive Behavior And Procrastination The Masterclass Ухоплан - Наилучшее настроение и интересный, универсальный контент в сети всегда актуально. https://uhoplan.ru/videokursy-audiokursy/477277-impulsive-behavior-and-procrastination-the-masterclass.html

https://www.dba-village.com/villa/wsvilla/r/dba-village/scripts?session=16628980260461 (search for 'aalok', you will find some of my work still out there from year 2003/2004)

Hiring Trends Index: a look at the recruitment landscape of Q1 2024 | Totaljobs. https://www.totaljobs.com/recruiter-advice/hiring-trends-index-a-look-at-the-recruitment-landscape-of-q1-2024

9 Things Authors Need to Know When Curating Their Instagram - SparkPress. https://gosparkpress.com/9-things-authors-need-to-know-when-curating-their-instagram/

Custom Microlearning Course Development Services. https://www.msnod.com/microlearning-development-services.html

Ultimate Entrepreneurship Lessons: An Extensive Guide | The Business Tycoon. https://thebusinesstycoonmagazine.com/ultimate-entrepreneurship-lessons/

Strategies for Overcoming Learning Challenges in the Workplace - Abakada Studios. https://www.abakadastudios.com/technology/strategies-for-overcoming-learning-challenges-in-the-workplace/

BOOKS INSPIRED ME

Bhagavad Gita As IT Is, A C Bhaktivedanta Swami Prabhupada

What are you doing with your life? J. Krishnamurti

Deep Work, Cal Newport

Atomic Habits – James Clear

Mindset – Dr. Carol Dweck

Man's Search for Meaning – Viktor Frankl

IKIGAI, Keira Miki

EAT THAT FROG!, Brian Tracy

The Mountain Is YOU, Brianna Wiest

Leading With Questions, Michael J. Marquardt

Life's Amazing Secrets, Gaur Gopal Das

Monday Blues to T . G . I . F, Uday V Doiphode

Say Less Get More, Fotini Iconomopoulous

Turn the Ship Around !, L. David Martquet

The Holy Science, Jannavatar Swami Sri Yukteswar Giri

The Voice of Babaji, V T Neelakantan, S A A Ramaiah , Bajaji Nagaraj

Who Moved My Cheese? Dr. Spencer Johnson

The Richest Man in Babylon, George S.Clason

GLOSSARY

The Glossary defines key terms from the book, making them accessible for Gen Z and Alpha readers new to the tech and career space.

Digital Hustle: Intentional, self-led career building in tech, focusing on adaptability and sustainability over traditional grind culture.

MAP Framework: A career navigation strategy focusing on Mindset (growth-oriented thinking), Adaptability (staying flexible), and Purpose (aligning work with personal values).

MIND MAP Resume: A personalized resume framework emphasizing Mindset, Intentionality, Navigation, and Discipline to highlight your unique tech journey.

Skill Stack: A diverse set of skills (hard and soft) that make you versatile in tech roles, more valuable than a job title.

Slow Hustle: A balanced approach to work, prioritizing recovery, and intentionality to prevent burnout.

Techno Translator: A professional with cross-functional fluency who can bridge coding, communication, and business domains.

Vibin': Gen Z slang for being in sync or harmony with your career path, feeling energized and aligned with your goals.

Building in Public: Sharing your tech journey (projects, failures, wins) on platforms like GitHub or LinkedIn to gain visibility and opportunities.

INDEX

The Index provides a quick reference to key topics, making it easy for readers to navigate the book's themes and concepts.

ABOUT THE AUTHOR

Aalok is a seasoned IT professional with over 24 years of experience working across four countries. He brings a rich global perspective to the evolving world of technology. His diverse journey—leading digital transformations—has shaped his deep understanding of what it truly takes to handle today's digital Hustle and build a sustainable career in IT.

With a passion for Coaching, mentoring, and empowering the Young generation, Aalok wrote this book as a practical guide for young professionals and aspiring techies who want more than just a job title—they want a purpose-driven path. Drawing from real-world stories, simple tools, and actionable techniques, *Art of Digital Hustle* reflects Aalok's mission: to help others convert passion into purpose and build a career that is not only successful but also self-aware and stress-resilient.

This book is the result of decades of research, self-discovery, and lessons learned on the front lines of the global tech industry. Now, Aalok shares it all—raw, honest, and ready—to inspire readers to take control, stay focused, be self-inspired, and thrive in the digital age.

9 798899 616181